Higgledy-Piggledy Stones:
Family Stories from
Ireland and Minnesota

Higgledy-Piggledy Stones: Family Stories from Ireland and Minnesota

by

Jannet L. Walsh

SHANTI ARTS PUBLISHING

BRUNSWICK, MAINE

Higgledy-Piggledy Stones:
Family Stories from Ireland and Minnesota

Published by Shanti Arts Publishing
Interior and cover design by Shanti Arts Designs

Shanti Arts LLC
193 Hillside Road
Brunswick, Maine 04011

shantiarts.com

All images are used with permission of the Walsh family.

This work depicts actual events in the life of the author as truthfully as
recollection permits and/or can be verified by research. Occasionally,
dialogue consistent with the character or nature of the person speaking
has been supplemented. All persons named within are actual individuals
who have either died, given permission for their name and story to be
shared, or had their name changed by the author to respect their privacy.

Printed in the United States of America

ISBN: 978-1-956056-71-6

Library of Congress Control Number: 2023934010

To Ellen Brennan Foley, my Great-Great-Grandmother, for immigrating from Ireland and helping establish the family's foundation in Minnesota one stone at a time; and to her descendants, for bettering the state of Minnesota by working the land and educating themselves and others.

Table of Contents

Acknowledgments _____ 9

Chronology _____ 11

Preface _____ 37

Ellen Brennan Foley _____ 45

Knockanarroor and the Milkman _____ 51

What's in a Name? _____ 55

Shelbourne Hotel Tea and Dad _____ 59

Civil War Solider James G. Foley _____ 65

Grandpa Martin _____ 69

Murdock on the Edge of the World _____ 85

Aunt Agnes's Curriculum Vita _____ 97

Aunt Margaret _____ 111

Irish Passport Stamp _____ 123

Bubbling Holy Well at Shrone City _____ 133

Irish Crosstown Cottage _____ 139

Finding Dromkerry _____ 155

Exile from Ireland: Irish Port of Cobh _____ 171

Tales of Two Dublins: Dublin Farm,

Dublin Fair City _____ 181

Epilogue _____ 197

About the Author _____ 205

Acknowledgments

*T*HIS COLLECTION OF STORIES IS ABOUT MY FAMILY and our stories; it splices known facts and knowledge, and what can be gathered through research, documents, interviews and visiting locations where my family is associated in Minnesota and Ireland.

I acknowledge first my family for sharing what little knowledge they could pass on to me through the generations since departing Ireland. It was at home in Murdock, Minnesota, I learned of our connections to the Catholic Colony in De Graff, Minnesota.

I owe, of course an immense debt to members of my family, both living and deceased. It is through their lives I want to make sense of our lives as a family, our exile from Ireland and settling in Swift County, Minnesota. A special tribute to my brother Paul M. Walsh for preparing our late father's 1953 Kodachrome slides of Martin J. Walsh Jr.'s travels to Ireland.

The Swift County Historical Society in Benson, Minnesota; Thomas Steman, University Archivist at St. Cloud State University; and the Minnesota Historical Society in St. Paul, all provided countless historical details to strengthen my research and findings.

My gratitude to Michael Lynch, Archivist at Kerry Library in Tralee, County Kerry, Ireland, for his help along the way to locate historical documents and field numerous questions. The National Library in Dublin genealogy experts, the staff of the Shelbourne Hotel in Dublin, who played a role in my research, and other people too numerous to mention, as well as strangers pointing me on the right path. My thanks also to genealogist Christy Keating at Cobh Heritage Centre, Cobh town, County Cork, Ireland, for providing information about Irish immigration before the Great Famine. Most precious are the family Civil War letters sent home to Minnesota, discovered by Ed and Colleen Foley at the National Archives, Washington, DC, 1991, for future generations to learn about earliest years of my family as Americans.

Olive and John Horgan, along with their entire family, of Crosstown, Killarney, helped me achieve my goal of finding the origins or my family in County Kerry, Ireland. Residents of Knockanarroor

Townland in County Kerry, the Fitzgerald and Sheehan families in Dromkerry, County Kerry, Ireland, along with Patrick and Margaret O Sullivan of Shamrock Cottage, from Black Valley, Gap of Dunloe, along with the parish of Our Lady of Black Valley. Special thanks to Kelly Boldan in Minnesota for helping me find family connections to Knockanarroor Townland, prompting me to visit Ireland in 2011, propelling future travel.

My gratitude extends to St. Cloud State University for financial support for travel and field work in Ireland, December 2018 and January 2019, not to mention collegial inspiration. My mentors at Augsburg University provided enthusiastic encouragement and wisdom to guide me along the way, culminating in this book.

To Cheryl Alberts Irwin, I express my gratitude for years of friendship, and continuously listening to my stories and adventures, trying to find the best way to deliver my family's story.

Sister Julitta Walsh wrote to me in 1984 when I was a student at St. Cloud State University, encouraging me to discover my roots, and tell my family's story. I am thankful I was able to pursue the most significant story I'll ever tell in my life.

Chronology

1820 Ellen Brennan is born to parents Michael Brennan and Margaret Daly, Dromkerry, County Kerry, Ireland.

1820–24 Margaret Daly of Dromkerry dies likely at birth of Ellen, or as late as 1824.

1822 William Foley is born in Ireland, birthplace unknown, but family folklore points to Killorglin, County Kerry, Ireland.

1824 Michael Brennan of Dromkerry marries Johanna Daly of Milltown in County Kerry, Ireland, and has four children born between 1827 and 1834.

1829 The Irish Penal Laws are repealed, and Irish Catholics are free to travel outside of Ireland.

1836 Ellen Brennan is sponsor at baptism of Charles Brenan [sic], Knockanarroor, County Kerry, Ireland.

1836–41 Ellen Brennan and William Foley depart Ireland by ship for Canada.

1841 Ellen Brennan and William Foley marry at St. Steven's Church, Milltown, New Brunswick, Canada.

1841–54 Ellen and William Foley move from Canada to Calais, Maine.

1845 Great Famine starts in Ireland due to failure of potato crops.

1846 Stephen Francis Foley is born in Calais, Maine, parents Ellen and William Foley.

1849–52 Great Famine ends in Ireland, one million Irish people die of starvation and related diseases during famine, and another million emigrate.

1854   Ellen and William Foley, along with children, travel by
        covered wagon drawn by oxen to Stillwater, Minnesota.
        Ellen and William build a sod home, and settle in Stillwater.

1862   James G. Foley, 19, enlists for volunteer duty during Civil
        War in United States Army with permission by his father,
        William Foley, Stillwater, Minnesota.

1876   Stephen F. Foley marries Catherine Meier, originally from
        Luxembourg, in Washington County, Stillwater, Minnesota.
        (Other spellings for Catherine's maiden name include Meir,
        Meirs, and Meyers.)

1876   Archbishop John Ireland establishes first Catholic colony
        in De Graff, Minnesota, the first of his extensive western
        Minnesota Catholic colonization efforts.

1876–77 The first grasshopper plague comes to the De Graff colony
        and area, destroying first two years of crops of settlers.

1878   Stephen and Catherine Foley take up residence on their
        homestead in Louriston Township, Chippewa County,
        Minnesota. William Foley, Stephen's father, guides his
        sons in the dark of night to Stephen's homestead using star
        navigation.

1883   Ellen Brennan Foley dies, wife of William Foley, Stillwater,
        Minnesota, January 18, 1883.

1886   Mary Jannet Foley is born, also known as Jennie Foley,
        March 23, 1886, Louriston Township, Chippewa County,
        Minnesota. Daughter of Stephen F. Foley and Catherine
        Meier. Married name, Jennie Foley Walsh, and Jennie
        Walsh.

1887   Martin J. Walsh Sr., born, February 19, 1887, son of Michael
        Walsh Jr. and Mary (Mc Ginty) Walsh, in shanty house in
        Dublin Township, Section 32, rural Murdock, Minnesota.

1897   William Foley, husband of Ellen Foley, dies, Stillwater,
        Minnesota, at home of his son, James G. Foley.

1913   Stephen F. Foley dies at home in Louriston Township, Chippewa County Minnesota, May 2, 1913.

1915   Martin J. Walsh Sr. marries Jennie Foley Walsh (daughter of Stephen and Catherine Meier Foley), November 4, 1915, at Sacred Heart Catholic Church, Murdock, Minnesota.

1916   Mary Agnes Walsh is born October 18, 1916, in a hotel in Murdock, Minnesota, daughter of Martin J. Walsh Sr. and Jennie Foley Walsh.

1917   Margaret Anne Walsh is born December 16, 1917, in a hotel in Murdock, Minnesota, daughter of Martin J. Walsh Sr. and Jennie Foley Walsh.

1921   Catherine Meier Foley dies at home in Louriston Township, Chippewa County Minnesota, January 4, 1921.

1922   Martin and Jennie Walsh, along with daughters Mary Agnes and Margaret Anne move to their first and only home, the Murphy House, Murdock, September 16, 1922.

1922   Irish Free State declared; civil war breaks out in Ireland.

1924   Martin J. Walsh Jr. is born, December 7, 1924, at home at the Murphy House, Murdock, son of Martin J. Walsh Sr. and Jennie Foley Walsh. He is father of Paul, David and Jannet Walsh.

1927   Margaret I. (Glieden)Walsh is born, October 9, 1927, rural Brooten Minnesota. She is mother of Paul, David and Jannet Walsh.

1942   Word War II—Mary Agnes Walsh is stationed in Santa Barbara, California, on active duty as member of U.S. Marine Corps when a Japanese submarine attacks an oil field along the coastline of the Pacific Ocean.

1953   Martin J. Walsh Jr. becomes first known family member to return to Ireland, also goes to Canada and France.

1961   Paul M. Walsh is born, parents Martin J. Walsh Jr. and
        Margaret I. (Glieden) Walsh, Rice Memorial Hospital,
        Willmar, Minnesota.

1962   David Martin Walsh is born July 23, 1962, parents Martin J.
        Walsh Jr. and Margaret I. (Glieden) Walsh, Rice Memorial
        Hospital, Willmar, Minnesota; dies August 9, 1962.

1964   Jannet L. Walsh is born, parents Martin J. Walsh Jr. and
        Margaret I. (Glieden) Walsh, Rice Memorial Hospital,
        Willmar, Minnesota.

1981   Jannet L. Walsh travels first time to Ireland with family
        visiting Dublin, Ring of Kerry, and Killarney in County
        Kerry.

1985   Jennie Foley Walsh dies, Willmar, Minnesota, February 26,
        1985, age 98.

1988   Martin J. Walsh Sr., dies, Willmar, Minnesota, January 15,
        1988, age 100.

1991   Ed and Colleen Foley discover Civil War letters of James G.
        Foley, son of William and Ellen Foley, National Archives,
        Washington, D.C., 1991.

2003   Mary Agnes Walsh Shopa dies November 7, 2003, Santa
        Barbara, California, buried at Riverside National Cemetery.

2008   Martin J. Walsh Jr. dies December 6, 2008, Duluth,
        Minnesota.

2010   Jannet L. Walsh moves home to Murdock from Florida, lives
        in Murphy House.

2011   Margaret I. (Glieden)Walsh dies, October 12, 2011, South
        Range, Wisconsin.

2013   Margaret Anne Walsh dies, Bethesda Heritage Center,
        Willmar, Minnesota, December 3, 2013.

2011   Jannet L. Walsh goes to Townland Knockanarroor in County
        Kerry, Ireland, searching for family history.

2014   Jannet L. Walsh goes again to Townland Knockanarroor in County Kerry, and visits Dublin.

2018–19 Jannet L. Walsh goes to Townland Dromkerry in County Kerry for first time, and Dublin, May-June 2018, and returns to Ireland, December 2018-January 2019.

2020–21 Jannet L. Walsh takes refuge at Murphy House in Murdock during global pandemic.

This is the only existing photograph of Ellen Brennan Foley, born near Killarney, County Kerry, Ireland, in 1820 and died in 1883 in Stillwater, Minnesota. She is the author's great-great-grandmother.

This full-length portrait of Martin J. Walsh Sr. dates to around 1925. He is the author's grandfather.

Grandparents Jennie Walsh (left) and Martin J. Walsh Sr. (right) with their only grandchildren: Jannet L. Walsh, held by her grandmother, and Paul M. Walsh, held by the children's mother, Margaret I. Glieden Walsh. [Photo by the children's father, Martin J. Walsh Jr., Murdock, Minnesota, 1964.]

Statue honoring Annie Moore and her two brothers who left Ireland from Cobh Harbour on December 20, 1891, and arrived in the United States on January 1, 1892. Annie was the first passenger to be processed at the newly opened Ellis Island immigration center in New York City. Cobh Harbour was the last view for many Irish who emigrated from Ireland.

Martin J. Walsh Sr. married Mary Jannet "Jennie" Foley (daughter of Stephen and Catherine Meier Foley), November 4, 1915, at Sacred Heart Catholic Church, Murdock, Minnesota.

Martin J. Walsh Sr., October 1922, age 35, shortly after he, wife, Jennie, and daughters, Mary Agnes and Margaret Anne, moved to their first and only home, the Murphy House, in Murdock, Minnesota.

Family of Stephen F. Foley and Catherine Meier Foley. Late 1890s, Louriston Township, Chippewa County, Minnesota. Back row: Mary Jannet "Jennie" Foley Walsh (author's grandmother); William Joseph Foley; John Marion Foley. Front row: James Daniel Foley; Catherine Meier Foley (author's great-grandmother, born in Luxembourg); Mary Agnes "Maime" Foley Walsh, Stephen Frances Foley (author's great-grandfather, born Calais, Maine); and Rose Ellen Foley Pothen.

Martin J. Walsh Sr., seated right, celebrates with his wife, Mary Jannet "Jennie" Foley Walsh, seated left, their 50th wedding anniversary, Murdock, Minnesota, 1965. Seated with the couple are their two grandchildren, Paul M. Walsh, age 4, and Jannet L. Walsh, age 1. Standing in second row, from right, Mary Agnes Walsh Shopa, Margaret I. (Glieden) Walsh, Martin J. Walsh Jr., and Margaret A. Walsh. The celebration was at the Murdock Village Hall, 1965.

A two-story wooden house with porch, family home of Martin J. (Sr.) and Jennie Walsh, 1940s. The porch is now enclosed to serve as windbreak during the harsh Minnesota winters. Fieldstones from an old flour mill previously located on this spot were used for the house foundation. The author's father, Martin J. Walsh Jr. was born at this home.

Martin J. Walsh Sr. (left standing), son of Michael J. (Jr.) and
Mary McGinty Walsh, married Mary Jannet "Jennie" Foley (left
seated), daughter of Stephen and Catherine Foley, on November
4, 1915, at Sacred Heart Catholic Church, Murdock, Minnesota.
The other couple is Henry L. Walsh (right standing), brother of
Martin, and Mary Agnes "Maime" Foley Walsh (right seated),
sister of Jennie. Henry and Maime married in 1919. The children
of the two couples are double cousins as they shared the same
grandparents, Michael J. and Mary Walsh, and Stephen and
Catherine Foley. It is not certain whose wedding was being
celebrated when this photograph was taken.

Margaret Anne Walsh, born December 16, 1917, left, and her sister, Mary Agnes Walsh, born October 18, 1916, pose for a photograph in Benson, Minnesota, June 1918. The girls were both born in a hotel in Murdock where they lived with their parents, Martin J. Walsh Sr. and Mary Jannet "Jennie" Foley Walsh.

Mary Agnes Walsh Shopa (left), about age ten with her sister, Margaret Anne Walsh, about age nine. Late 1920s. Murdock, Minnesota.

Margaret A. Walsh as a student at St. Cloud Teachers College, 1935–1939, where she was studying to be a school teacher.

Mary Jannet "Jennie" Foley Walsh was rolling bandages for the war effort when this photograph was taken in Murdock, Minnesota, sometime between 1915 and 1917.

This is the US Passport of Martin J. Walsh Jr., 1953, with US immigration stamp, New York, June 2, 1953.

This is a view of the filling station run by Jack Clarke, foreground, with of view of Murdock, Minnesota, with the Great Northern Railway station next to the railroad tracks and grain elevators. Photo is from a black and white slide by Martin J. Walsh Jr.

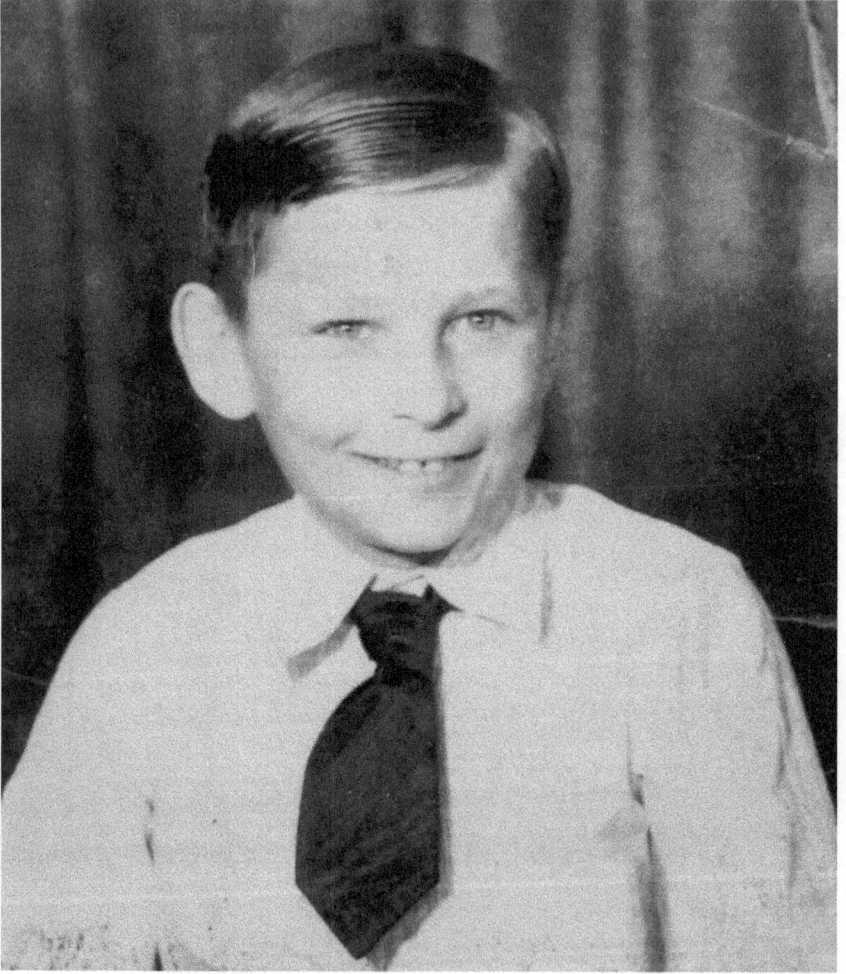

This is a grade school portrait of Martin J. Walsh Jr., about age nine, Murdock, Minnesota. He is the author's father.

This is a portrait of Martin J. Walsh Jr., son of Martin Sr., and Jennie Walsh, born at home in Murdock, Minnesota, 1924. He is the author's father.

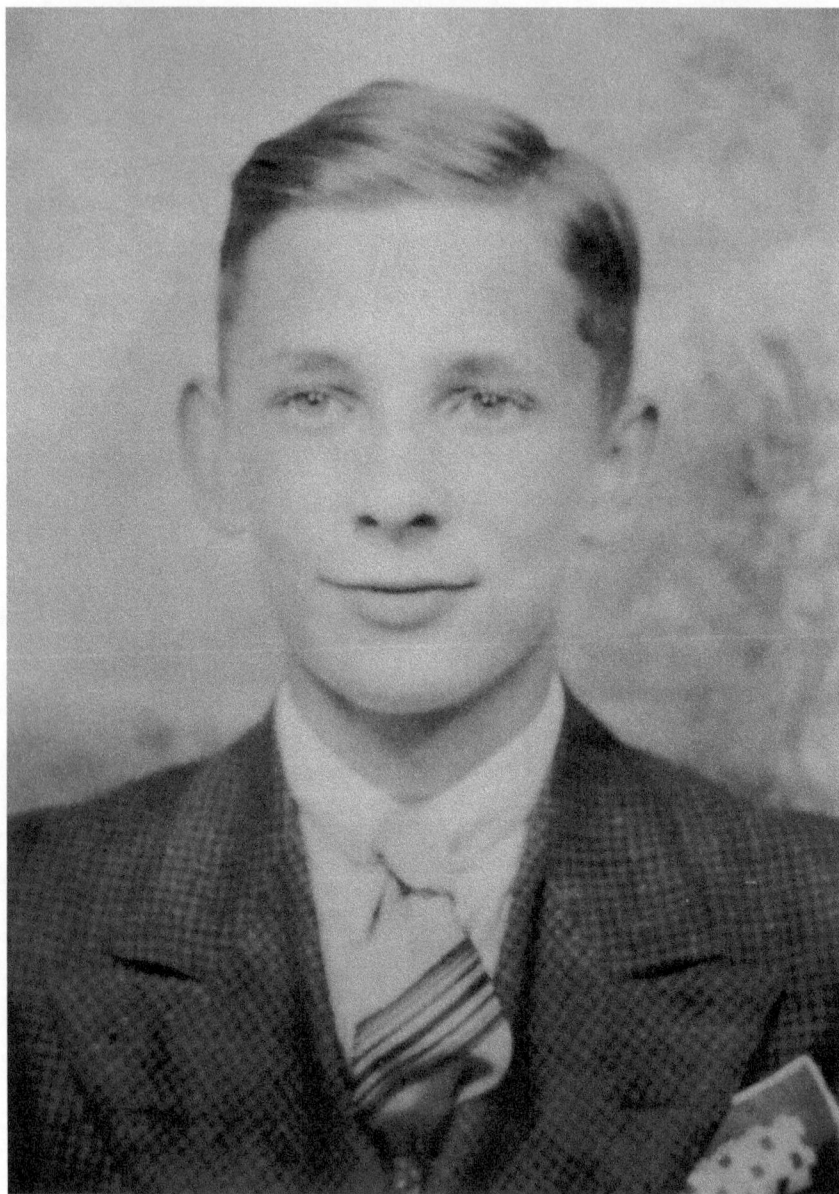

This photograph of Martin J. Walsh Jr. was likely taken to mark high school graduation around 1942.

Mary Agnes Walsh, known to family as Agnes, served during World War II as a Corporal in the US Marine Corps. She was stationed in Santa Barbara, California, in 1942 when a Japanese submarine attacked an oil field along the coastline of the Pacific Ocean.

Preface

O**N A COLD JANUARY DAY IN 2011, I FOUND A BLACK-**
and-white portrait of Ellen hidden away in a yellowed pillowcase
tucked inside a plastic floral shopping bag deep in an attic closet at my
home in Murdock, Minnesota, population 278. I can only guess that the
portrait and other family artifacts were waiting patiently to be revealed
at the appropriate time, maybe even to the right person, having been
previously set in place by the earlier keeper of family archives, Aunt
Margaret. A handwritten card gave hints about the photograph, calling
me to active duty as family historian. I was already deeply entrenched
in this task, living as I did on top of layers of pioneers and immigrants
from Ireland, Canada, and other lands.

Ellen Brennan, who married William Foley, is my great-great-
grandmother, born in 1820 in rural County Kerry, Ireland, near
Killarney town. She emigrated to North America between 1836 and
1841, first to Canada, then settling in the United States. She died in
1883 and is buried in Bayport, Minnesota, an almost eight-foot-tall
granite memorial commemorating her life. It is Ellen's birth and
baptismal record that led me to Dromkerry Townland in 2018. The
Catholic parish of Milltown, along with the Killagha Abbey, is the site
of a former monastery started by St. Colman in the seventh century.
Until then, information about Ellen's origins was lost in time for
almost two hundred years.

In 2010, I left Florida, where I worked in photojournalism and
public relations, returning home to tiny Murdock to live in a little
house my family has called home for almost one hundred years. I
moved home to the heart of my family and the headquarters of family
history, to the open prairies and soil of the people of the earth—
farmers. Ellen's photo prompted me to travel in April 2011 to Ireland,
specifically Townland Knockanarroor, a rural farming community
near Killarney town in County Kerry. Ellen was a sponsor to a baptism
in Knockanarroor in 1836, a fact that shed light on a possible place
of origin for my family. With two very specific locations in Ireland
associated with my family, down to precise unmarked farm roads, I
hit pay dirt in my Irish genealogy search.

The 2011 trip to Ireland was followed by four more in the search for bits and pieces of information about the people, land, and culture cast aside by my ancestors. I didn't understand it at the time of my travels, but I was on a quest, traveling by airplane nearly thirty thousand miles total round trip from Minneapolis, Minnesota, to Shannon Airport or Dublin Airport, between 2011 and 2019. I challenged myself to drive in Ireland on the left side of the road as I needed to travel the countryside to remote locations and numerous unmarked roads to try to uncover my family's past. I knew I could only be satisfied by walking where my family lived, worked, worshiped, and died. It could be that I had this desire to make sense of lost lives, lost memories, and needed to tell my story as part of a larger story of my family's past, not just for myself, but other family members wanting to put the pieces of history in order.

My quest to understand my family's roots started sometime as a child in the 1970s, listening to my father Martin J. Walsh Jr. tell stories to family members gathered in the living room of my grandparent's home in Murdock, the very same house I now call home. I was the little girl sitting on the floor wearing thick, heavy prescription eye glasses and red braided hair, often sporting one of my mother's sewing creations, patterned on McCall's or Simplicity designs and stitched with a 1950s Necchi Supernova sewing machine. In this living room scene, a Great Northern or Burlington Northern freight train traveled down the tracks outside the front door, with only the road and a ditch as a divider. Conversations would be halted with the sounds of train whistles from the locomotive approaching the railroad crossing, and until the last rattle of the caboose was far from view and earshot.

The people that day, seated on the sofa and stuffed chairs, are just shadows in my mind, almost all deceased, but the moment left an impression of what was very important to my father, and is very important to me today. I can still see my father holding in his hands copies of the United States citizenship papers of my great-grandfather Michael John Walsh Jr., born in Canada, and my great-great-grandfather, Michael John Walsh Sr., born in Ireland, signing their names with their mark of "X," renouncing loyalties to Ireland and the Queen of England, at a time when Ireland was still under English rule.

It was also at this time that I understood my family was part of Bishop John Ireland's people, mainly poor Irish immigrants, who were hand selected by the religious leader to live in De Graff, Minnesota, located in Swift County, the first in a series of Catholic colonies in Minnesota. Ireland was bishop, 1884 to 1888, later appointed first archbishop of the Diocese of Saint Paul, 1888 to 1918, holding a significant place in Minnesota's pioneering history.

For some reason, at the age of eight, nine, or ten years old, I understood my family came from an island far away called Ireland; that we had to leave because of food shortages, and were sent as farmers to make our way in rural Minnesota. I still remember the confusion as a girl learning a bishop was named after the same island country, Ireland, my family came from. Today, I live three miles from De Graff, a location that once had plans to have a small Catholic college and a normal school for training teachers, and where many descendants of the original families of the De Graff colony still continue to work together in the fields at harvest and planting seasons, pray on Sundays together, stand as pallbearers at funerals, and continue to give help and support to the newest wave of immigrants in Murdock, now mainly from Mexico, working in the dairies owned by my relatives.

The Catholic Church of St. Bridget, founded in De Graff in 1876, displays a mission statement by the main entrance, referring to the faith community. Although there are no details about the selection process for the settlers in De Graff, I am very fortunate to see the hard work my ancestors endured in their first years in Swift County continues today. This is the inscription:

"We, the community of believers of St. Bridget's Parish, De Graff, Minnesota, were chosen in 1876 by Archbishop Ireland to bring the Gospel to the new territory and its people. The pioneers dedicated themselves to serving God and God's Family.

"Parishioners today carry on the traditions of the early settlers, who in their staunch faith, reached out to those in need. We work together to become a spirit-filled community woven in faith by the Eucharist and the Word.

"We strive to be steadfast stewards of the soil. We are committed to the growth of our members, young and old. We serve God through our ministries of support, music, education and gatherings.

"Throughout our journey and with the love of Jesus, we bring God's people together in Christian Unity."

A broader view of Archbishop Ireland's plan in the nineteenth century helped resettle about four thousand Catholic families in west central and southwestern Minnesota, 1875–1885, resulting in establishing villages in five counties (Swift, Nobles, Murray, Big Stone, and Lyon Counties) in Minnesota, with De Graff and Clontarf in Swift County as the first efforts for resettlement for Minnesota Catholic colonization. The heart of the Archbishop's goal with resettlement included alleviating the perceived problems of nativist prejudice or anti-immigrant sentiment, anti-Catholicism, poverty and loss of religion faced by urban Catholics, particularly Irish on the east coast in the United States, and poor Catholics still in Ireland by relocating them to low-cost farmlands in western Minnesota.

Although these Minnesota Catholic colonies were designed for the poor, it does not mean immigrants could come empty handed, according to the National Register of Historic Places Inventory—Nomination Form for the Church of St. Bridget, 1985. Archbishop Ireland suggested no settlers should move west without at least $400 in hand, but needed more to get started in order to have a minimum level of comfort and money to purchase farm machinery. These settlers were offered land as low as $1.40 an acre, and the Catholic priest Father F. J. Swift, the first resident pastor at De Graff (1876–1879), served as land agent when not saying Mass or looking after his flock of souls, and also helped arrange loans and accommodations in the local immigration house when settlers were breaking their first five acres of land.

Expenditures for housing, or poor man's temporary house, cost about $38.75, including lumber, two windows, two doors and shingles, measuring about sixteen by eighteen feet. Another option for housing included a portable house for $200, fourteen by twenty feet, offering a frame house said to be rain, wind, and waterproof, as well as hurricane proof, with a living room, kitchen, and bedroom. These prefabricated houses were made in Chicago, brought to settlers by rail and if painted regularly, would last for a century.

❧

When I was in my junior year at St. Cloud State University, fall 1984, I wrote one of my relatives, a Catholic religious sister, the late Sister Julitta Walsh, CSJ (Congregation of the Sisters of St. Joseph), working for the Diocese of Nashville, Nashville, Tennessee. I was working on a project for my American Studies course with Professor Emeritus William Morgan about my family history. It was Sister Julitta who interviewed my grandfather Martin J. Walsh Sr., August 12, 1976, to record oral history in celebration of the bicentennial of the United States.

Grandpa said during the interview a house was moved out from De Graff by his grandfather Michael (Michael Walsh Sr., my great-great-grandfather). It was a shanty house Grandpa Martin was born in, February 19, 1887, in Dublin Township, Section 32. This land is located in Swift County, next to Chippewa County to the south. Shortly after birth, the family moved to Section 34, where his father Michael Walsh Jr. farmed, later Henry L. Walsh, Grandpa Martin's brother, followed by Henry's son, Henry J. Walsh, known to family as Young Henry. Grandpa referred to the farm in Section 34 as Henry's farm in 1976, as this type of informal naming of farms was common practice for conversation, and the same goes today here in Dublin Township.

In 1984 I was staying in Shoemaker Hall on campus in St. Cloud when I first read the letter from Sister Julitta handwritten on official stationery from Diocese of Nashville. She sent me a copy of her typewritten transcript of the 1976 interview she did of my Grandpa, and also enclosed the letter I wrote her. As I look at the letter dated September 12, 1984, from Sister Julitta, she writes to say she is delighted to hear I am undertaking the project of tracing my family roots as she was vitally interested in the same, but wasn't in the position to pursue. She asks me to keep her informed of my progress.

Sister Julitta made a good impression on me, maybe more than I know. I can still see her talking with the ladies, not wearing a habit or veil, in the kitchen here in Murdock when she was home for visits, now my kitchen. Now if I could only tell her of all my findings as Sister Julitta died in 2015 at the age of ninety-two. Almost four decades have passed since I wrote Sister Julitta to tell a story about my family, perhaps the most significant story I will ever tell in my life. I've kept her letter locked away for years, carrying it to all the places I called home, referring back to it often, as I always thought I might be able to continue my quest when the time was right.

※

Author James Patrick Shannon, in "Catholic Colonization on the Western Frontier," states that expenditures for farm implements and draft oxen were also needed by prairie settlers, with a yoke of oxen weighing about 3,200 to 3,400 pounds for $100; a breaking plow, $23, required to cut through virgin prairie land; and a wagon, $75; for a total of $198. Estimates for feeding a family of four and heating their house for a year included thirty bushels of wheat, ground into flour, $30; groceries, $15; one cow for milk, $25; and fuel for heating, $30; totaling $100.

Settlers started arriving in De Graff in 1876, establishing farms. Most were born in Ireland, or were children of parents born in Ireland. Just one year after De Graff was established, there was a train depot, flour mill, brick yard, four general stores, two hardware stores, two blacksmiths, a hotel and an emigrant house, according to information from the Swift County Historical Society.

My quest to make sense of the Ireland my family left behind before the Great Famine, and put the pieces together of their lives as pioneers in North America, started years ago, but escalated in recent years as digital and online documents became easier to access. Before the Internet, this search had to be conducted in person, at libraries, churches, and museums, most accessible only with travel.

I carry the family's torch to understand my Irish ancestors, yet I am 100 percent American, with a mixture of known nationalities including German, Prussian, Luxembourgian, Scottish, and Canadian. Canada was home to many of my Irish ancestors before they arrived in the United States, such as William Foley and Ellen Brennan Foley, and my Walsh family. My affinity to my Irish ancestors includes my red hair, although even that is likely the result of the Vikings raiding, trading, and settling in Ireland. My last name—Walsh—is clearly from Ireland; it means "of the Welsh people from Wales, settling in Ireland," which suggests I may have ancestors in Wales.

The family crest of Walsh hangs in the kitchen—unofficial family headquarters—at home in Murdock, a souvenir from my first visit to Ireland in 1981. The walls of the simple, two-story white wooden house have witnessed births and deaths, including my baby brother David Martin Walsh, 1962, who lived less than a month. The location of the little white house is often described by my family as the second house from the west end of Murdock on US Highway 12, and one house away from Sacred Heart Catholic Cemetery, separated by Dooley's Garage. The little white house has been a safe harbor for my family and visitors during the Great Depression, the 1940 Armistice Day blizzard, World War II, assassination of President John F. Kennedy; and my place to return to in 2010, surviving the Great Recession and job layoffs, after living in Florida for more than a decade. My house now adds the pandemic starting in 2020 to its historical list.

My father, Martin J. Walsh Jr., nicknamed Marty to avoid confusion with his father, Martin J. Walsh Sr., with a nickname of Mart, made our family's first known return trip home to Ireland in 1953, recording his adventures with Kodachrome color slides and his Clarus 35mm camera, leaving behind traces for me to follow in Canada, Ireland, and France. I imagine him as a very proud young man with the incredible opportunity to see the homeland of his great-grandmother Ellen. He didn't have a chance to locate the dirt farm roads I discovered in Dromkerry, looking out at the Gap of Dunloe, the Lakes of Killarney, the MacGillycuddy's Reeks, and Purple Mountain ranges, some of the most beautiful views in all of Ireland. It has been an honor to have had the opportunity to walk where my family walked and lived, to catch any whispers of their voices from the difficult times in Ireland's history, when people survived day by day. There is no evidence my family owned land in Ireland, but were certainly tenants of Irish Protestant gentry who owned large land masses, established by their loyalty to England.

In 1829 my family was just starting to openly practice their faith as Roman Catholics. This was after Catholic politician Daniel O'Connell's campaign for Catholic emancipation, which restored basic civil rights to Catholics, ending the penal laws that prevented Catholics in Ireland from owning land, practicing the Catholic religion, receiving an education, holding public office, or traveling outside of Ireland.

I never heard my grandparents Martin and Jennie Walsh speak the Irish language. My brother Paul learned a few details from our Aunt Agnes about Grandpa Martin during our trip to Ireland in 1981. Paul said, "I remember Agnes saying as we were listening to the Irish speak in Ireland: 'If you listen, you can hear the similarity in the accent that Grandpa still had, as he spoke with a slight Irish accent.'" It's likely my family stopped speaking Irish scores of years ago during the penal years when it was prohibited by the British, but I will never be certain. Today the Irish language is recognized as an official working language in the European Union. Shamrocks, shenanigans, and shillelaghs are some of the few Irish words I learned as a child, but later I was fortunate to receive basic training in the Irish language by Olive Horgan while I was staying at Crosstown Cottage, near Killarney, County Kerry, Ireland. Unfortunately, I can't carry on a conversation in Irish, and desperately need more language lessons for future visits to Ireland.

Few oral histories or written sagas follow the specific journey of my family as emigrants from Ireland, before settling in the United States. My collection of essays and a few poems will help to serve as a legacy to future generations interested in information I have gathered about my Irish roots, setting off another generation of questers.

My Irish ancestors inspired me to write this book, pointing me to Ellen's rural County Kerry, Ireland. There was a great force that propelled Ellen to depart Ireland as a young woman and led her to make a new life in North America. Yet I have no details, no shipboard records, only what I have managed to piece together in my research. I can't answer why my family's stories of Ireland were not shared or are forgotten, undoubtedly like so many who left their pasts behind to come to the new country. It could be Ellen's departure was the same as a death in order to survive in a new world; perhaps she needed to forget as all energies were in day-to-day survival. My desire to recover the landscapes and places dear to Ellen has become vital to me, now part of my life, and my story. I want to understand Ellen's pain and suffering as an Irish emigrant, and to tell the forgotten stories of my Irish ancestors that I did not hear as a child.

My mother always made sure I wore a green shamrock pin on St. Patrick's Day, almost always saying because I was Irish, but the next sentence would always follow that she was not Irish. As little girl, I would question why she wasn't Irish, but it would be the same story, my father was Irish, therefore I was. I am fairly certain I was dressed in a kilted skirt to add to my cultural Irish dress, especially during elementary school.

As of 2019, I have visited Dublin, Ireland, at least five times. At the end of the trip to Dublin in January 2019, I wanted to go home to Minnesota. I wanted to go home to Dublin Township in Swift County. I wanted to go home to Murdock where I first heard my family was part of Archbishop Ireland's people. I wanted to go home to the kitchen headquarters and drink tea, and stand in the living room where my father told me of my Irish roots. I am an American first, yet know I am part of the island of Ireland as my ancestors are now resting in unmarked graves piled with stones.

Chapter 1

Ellen Brennan Foley

EPITAPH OF ELLEN BRENNAN FOLEY
Sacred to the memory of
Wife of William Foley
Born in Killarney, County of Kerry, Ireland
May 15, 1820
Died January 18, 1883

Around her loved and honored grave, The severed household band may
come, And seem to hear those blessed tones, that made the music of our
home. The faded form, the silent shroud, these, these were all we gave the
tomb. She watches o'er us, while she wears, the freshness of immortal bloom.
—St. Michael's Cemetery, Bayport, Minnesota
Transcription by Mary Elizabeth-Dolan Angstman

THESE WORDS ARE INSCRIBED IN THE SANDSTONE memorial to Ellen Brennan Foley, my great-great- grandmother, almost unreadable by the human eye at St. Michael's Cemetery in Bayport, Minnesota. The engraving has deteriorated since Ellen's death in 1883. Countless snowstorms and extreme weather conditions in Bayport, a short distance from the scenic bluffs of the St. Croix River, eroded the stone. Ellen is buried next to her husband William Foley and several members of their family; some grave markers are missing and others are not legible. The Foley family is part of more than 7,000 internments since the cemetery opened in 1873, serving the Catholic churches of St. Michael's in Bayport and St. Mary's in Stillwater.

Ellen Brennan and William Foley were married August 31, 1841, at St. Stephen's Catholic Church, Milltown, New Brunswick, Canada, according to Charlotte County records, marriage record RS148. The Canadian handwritten marriage record reads as follows: "William Foley of the parish of Saint Stephen's and Ellen Brennan of the same parish were married by banns with consent of parents this thirty-first day of August in the year of our Lord one thousand eight hundred and forty-one (1841) by me Jon Commins, Priest. This marriage was solemnized between William Foley, in presence of Cornelius Finn [his X mark], Mary Ann Brennan [her X mark]. Rec & Req 11 Dec 1841."

Ellen is buried a short distance from the St. Croix River in Bayport, Minnesota, but a different St. Croix River also flows through the Foley story. After Ellen and William married in Canada, they crossed the St. Croix River that forms part of the international border between the Canadian province of New Brunswick and the state of Maine. The couple lived in Calais, Maine, at least from 1841 to 1854. From Maine, they traveled by covered wagon drawn by oxen to Stillwater, Washington County, Minnesota, where they built a sod home.

In 2011, the first glimpse of locating a more precise location for Ellen Brennan Foley's origins became possible with online Irish Roman Catholic records. On November 1, 1836, Ellen Brennan was a sponsor at the baptism of Charles Brenan (spelled with one 'n' in the record) of Knockanarroor, a townland located about five miles east of Killarney town. The Catholic Parish of Glenflesk was the location of the baptism. Parents of the child are James Brenan and Mary Walsh. The other sponsor listed is Denis Sullivan. No relationship is listed for Ellen to Charles. Discoveries made in 2018 provided more leads in learning about Ellen's origins.

February 2018
St. Michael's Cemetery
Bayport, Minnesota

I am making a pilgrimage in the snow to visit Ellen's grave in Bayport, Minnesota. Cloven hoof prints of deer mark a snowy one-track road, while deer tracks also weave between graves and trees. I walk in snow drifts at least to my knees. The sky is overcast; temperature is 28 degrees. My notebook and pens are tucked in a large pocket of my warmest storm parka, ready to capture my thoughts. I talk to Ellen, seeking inspiration about her hidden Irish past.

Sacred Snowy Cemetery Pilgrimage

I pay a winter visit to you, Ellen Foley and family.
Here the earth is covered with a pure white blanket.

In this place my voice is sent direct to you.
Please let me begin with my notebook and pen.

Dearest Ellen, A fool you must think of your great-great-granddaughter standing deep in the snow. Snow is to my knees in places as I make my way to your eight-foot-high memorial.

I have visited before, asked you questions.

From Killarney you were born and raised,
married and lived in Canada,
gave birth to children in Maine,
traveled by cart pulled by oxen to Minnesota,
but in Stillwater you made your departure.

Do you hear the motor running? Grave diggers are preparing a new gravesite, taking down a green tent for mourners. Today a new resident joins you, just to the north, near the entrance.

Ellen, now I am asking for your wisdom. What say you of courage and strength? You left a life behind in the old sod, never to return to the island of forty shades of green. How did you bear the pain of leaving behind Ireland?

I see you as a very young woman departing on a pony and trap, past cottages with peat smoke puffing from chimneys. Tears and fears must have been heavy on your heart, waving goodbye for the last time to your parents.

In the shadow of the MacGillycuddy's Reeks you were born. From your family farm peat was cut from the bogs to use for cooking and heating. Butter churned in your cottage, taken to market.

Cows grazed in the pasture, surrounded by shades of green. You attended the horses at the carriage stop. Daily you milked cows.

What did you hide in your baggage on the ship to Canada? Was it photographs, flowers, Rosary beads, handkerchiefs, and a bundle of hope?

The landscape of your homeland is rich, but too poor to nourish and sustain. You departed Ireland to escape with your life. Ireland before the Great Famine gave life to generations. What were your thoughts while packing your bags? How many Hail Marys did you pray until you drifted to sleep at night?

To your new resident, just to the north, please point out the splendor of deer roaming in the snow.

Ice covers the St. Croix, the same river your husband William worked as a logger. No timber floats down the river today, yet the views remain spectacular.

My winter pilgrimage to your column of pink granite and sandstone is a first. Next time I will bring my snowshoes to walk above the snow. Before I take my leave, a Hail Mary I will pray.

Dearest Ellen and family, until my next visit.
I let you rest again peacefully in your sacred earth, covered in your thick blanket of snow.

I must travel home in the snowstorm. Please watch over me.

Jannet

June 2018
Minnesota State Archives
St. Paul, Minnesota

Armed with only a yellow legal notebook and a pencil, I place my order at the Minnesota Historical Society in St. Paul, Minnesota, for the *Stillwater Birth and Death Registers, 1871–1886*. On my library table rests a large white card with the number one, making it easy for the archives staff to deliver the two volumes that document Ellen Brennan Foley's death. The volumes are very large, about two feet by three feet, delivered by a cart, and placed in a large box. I open the box, find the needed volume, look first at birth records, and then flip the heavy book to the Register of Deaths, City of Stillwater.

At first, I can't understand the order of the records, then find Ellen B. Foley listed on page 14, No. 150. The date of death is January 18, 1883, followed by female, married, age sixty-two. Place of birth is listed only as Ireland—no city, townland, or county. The cause of death is rheumatism of heart. Occupation is none, yet she was certainly a housewife and mother. Her parents are listed as William and Mary Brennan from Ireland, no other details mentioned. I am not sure of the accuracy as my research in Ireland pointed to other possibilities. It is important to note that records, such as death certificates and other documents, are only records; the facts might not be what appears in the artifacts, though everything is important in the search to uncover the facts of a family's history.

In 2018, Michael Lynch, archivist at Kerry Library in Tralee, County Kerry, Ireland, emailed me regarding his discovery of an Ellen Brennan baptized in Milltown Catholic Parish on May 12, 1820. Her parents are listed as Michael Brennan and Margaret Daly, of Townland Droumkerry, modern spelling, Dromkerry. Sponsors John and Margaret are shown without last names. Ellen's grave gives her birth date as May 15, 1820. Lynch suggests that it wasn't so much that the discrepancy was not of concern, more that it was not sufficient to rule out this Ellen as the correct one; an itinerant priest taking notes might not always be accurate.

"Unless you are 100 percent sure that Knockanarroor is correct, this is a possibility for Ellen's origin, not for the coincidence, but also in the fact of her marrying a Foley, one of the most common surnames in the Milltown and Killorglin area," wrote Lynch.

Milltown is a name that's repeated in Ellen's history as she was married in Milltown, New Brunswick, Canada. The neighboring town of Killorglin in County Kerry is famous for the Puck Fair, a festival of a goat that is king for a day each year. My family's folklore says that Killorglin was the home of William Foley, but there is no actual proof. The burial grounds of Dromavally, located on the edge of Killorglin, is filled with numerous Foley gravesites.

Here is how the pieces of the story come together in my mind. Michael Brennan (the spelling of the last name varies) of Townland Dromkerry married Johanna Daly of Milltown on March 2, 1824, four years after Ellen's birth. It is likely that Margaret either died giving birth to Ellen or at some point in the first four years of Ellen's life. Johanna may have been a sister or a cousin of Margaret Daly, but there's no likelihood of knowing. Michael Brennan had a total of five children: one, Ellen, with Margaret Daly, and four with Johanna Daly—Timothy, Michael, Mary, and Margaret. James Brenan, father of Charles, for whom Ellen was a baptismal sponsor, was likely Michael Brennan's brother and, therefore, Ellen's uncle; Charles then was Ellen's cousin, but remains unknown.

The Brennan family in Dromkerry were tenants of Henry Arthur Herbert who owned Dromkerry and about 342 acres. The Herbert family owned the large Mucross House, an estate near Killarney, which hosted Queen Victoria in 1861.

With all of this information, I was confident that Michael Brennan and Margaret Daly were Ellen Brennan Foley's parents, and Ellen was from Townland Dromkerry near Milltown. Ellen likely worked in Knockanarroor, a stagecoach stop on the Irish butter roads with a place to exchange horses for the carriages, including a coach house next to the road; parts of the stone steps remain in ruins today, giving a glimpse of the past.

Still unsure of all the pieces, Lynch reassured me that this is what genealogy is, and there isn't always a solution to the missing pieces or fragments of history. The artifacts were before me, and I needed to make some order as best I could. "You have hit pay dirt. You came away with information on Brennan and Foley," said Lynch.

Chapter 2

Knockanarroor and the Milkman

IT IS APRIL 2011. I AM DRIVING A CAR WITH THE steering wheel on the right side while traveling on the left side of a rural highway east of Killarney, Ireland, looking for a safe place to turn into a petrol station near the village of Barraduff. I need to ask at the station for help locating an unmarked road where my family might have lived until the 1840s. The location I am seeking is Knockanarroor Townland, pronounced "Knock-on-a-roar" in Irish, meaning the hill of corn.[1]

I am quickly introduced to a milkman named Patrick "Pa" Brosnan, very familiar with local farms, by a petrol station attendant, and Patrick agrees to show me the way to the unmarked townland road. He instructs me to follow his lorry, a truck, or thought I was doing just that. What are my chances of following the wrong milkman on a rural road in Ireland? Apparently, the chances are high, as I started following the wrong milkman to the wrong farm, luckily, just less than a mile away. I am in the land County Kerry, made famous for milk production and connected to the prehistoric butter roads, paths used for transporting butter in the rough and mountainous region.

Waiting patiently along the side of the road, parked at the wrong farm, I watch for milkman Patrick to come to my rescue. Holding on tight to my maps, wondering what I had done and if I would find Knockanarroor, Patrick pulls his lorry near my rental car. He was not wearing an official dairy uniform, instead dresses casually wearing a tan and brown sweater with a zippered collar, denim trousers, and sporting a hint of a dark red or brown hair. Pointing with his left hand and holding my maps in his right hand, Patrick says, "It's on this way toward Barraduff, a half a mile."

---

1.   The country of Ireland has two official languages in Constitution, English and Irish. The Irish call their language in Irish Gaeilge, sounds similar to gail-gyuh. I first heard the word Gaeilge while visiting Knockanarroor, spoken to me by a resident. https://irishlanguage.nd.edu/about/what-is-irish

"I've missed the road turnoff?" I reply, wondering what insanity I had entered.

"Yes, you have missed the road turnoff," said Patrick. We are both laughing, but I still need to get to the place my family called home, forgotten for a few hundred years or so.

I boldly ask Patrick if he would get into my car and help guide me to Knockanarroor, like a ship needing a tug boat to reach the harbor safely. He agrees to join my adventure as I drive back to the petrol station in order to turn around, putting the car back on the road driving west to Killarney, about a mile before taking a turn north to the unmarked road. A few stones, ruins of steps, can be seen on the edge of the road, once used for passengers to board horse-drawn carriages.

Slowly I drive on the dirt townland road with grass growing down the center in patches, passing by ruins of homes built with stones. I am now feeling the excitement of a child. Patrick tells me to keep driving until we reach the end of the road, passing a few houses occupied with residents, along with ruins of cottages.

The milkman had traveled this road several times, picking up fresh milk from a farmer in Knockanarroor, delivering it to a nearby Cadbury chocolate factory in Rathmore. With processing at the factory, about twenty miles away, the milk was mixed with sugar and cocoa, transformed into chocolate bars in Dublin, and finally sent around the world.

When I reach the end of the road, I roll down the car window to talk with two men working on a stone fence in front of a nicely kept cottage. I ask, "Is this Knockanarroor?" Everyone is laughing and repeating my question, Patrick enjoys his adventure. I finally hear one of the men say genuinely and with calm, "This is Knockanarroor."

This is my opportunity to understand a little better the location my Irish ancestors left behind due to food shortages and other reasons long forgotten. The land in Knockanarroor is referred to by residents as a "poorish land" of wetlands, surrounded by bogs. The peat or turf, decayed vegetation, is cut and dried for heating and cooking fuel today, like my ancestors did with smoke puffing out of their cottage chimney, producing a musty smell. My exact connections to Knockanarroor are not easily defined, but it's likely my family served as grooms tending to the horses exchanged on the carriage route at the end of the road of Knockanarroor, on a major route to Killarney, now marked by a stone wall.

When I told my story later about how the milkman helped me find

Knockanarroor, I was quizzed by local Killarney residents, wanting to know his name, maybe to verify my crazy story of the milkman. I replied it was Patrick Brosnan from nearby Muckross. Local Killarney residents almost all said they knew him and he came from a good family, good people. Patrick was a milkman and a gentleman.

The hill of corn, and stones mark the entrance to my family's possible roots. I found a possible way home to Knockanarroor, and my possible Irish origins.

Firkins of Butter
On the Butter Road, Written in Murdock, 2018

The ancients buried butter in the bogs,
preserved in Ireland's peat fields.

This morning I open a tub of butter
at home in Minnesota,
imported from Ireland,
and smeared on my toast.

Firkins of butter, half a hundred weight each,
travel from Killarney to Cork Butter Exchange,
by horse and cart,
placed on ships,
sent out from cottages to the globe.

From the Hill of the Corn,
Knockanarroor,
Muckross House,
Rathmore and Glenflesk,
over the Gap of Dunloe,
past the Serpents Lake,
all Butter Roads lead to Ireland's seaport in Cork.

In the open-hearth kitchens,
women folk run the churn with cream,
until it breaks to butter.
And from the small farms,
Kerry milk cows still deliver milk daily.

Butter to gold, was the cash of the day.
Bartered in Cork by summer,
set in provisions for winter.

If no butter is made, the fairies are to blame
offering of cream and butter in cottages
for the mysterious creatures.

Did fairies travel with Ellen
in her hand baggage
to Canada seeking butter?
There's no word,
but Irish butter continues
to spread around the globe.

Why Irish butter?
It's of course not green, instead gold,
salted for preservation.
Tasty for cottage dwellers and nobles alike.

The Kerry cows grazing next to the parish church in Glenflesk,
simply as they please,
can't stop chewing their cud twice all day,
thank God.

Spread, melted, drizzled, a knuckle of butter heaven sent.

I'll have another slice of toast.
Please pass the butter.

Chapter 3

What's in a Name?

Diary entries from my late grandfather, Martin J. Walsh Sr., Murdock
January 5, 1964: "Peggy went in Rice Hospital. Martin and Paul here. We
now have one grandson and one granddaughter. Weather was mild."
January 6, 1964: "Girl born in Willmar, born 11 am. No name yet."
January 13, 1964: "Seventeen below overnight, no snow. Peggy went home
from Rice Hospital. Martin, Peggy, Paul, and baby to Litchfield."

I AM THAT BABY GIRL, BORN IN WILLMAR, MINNESOTA,
at Rice Hospital, receiving the name of Jannet, named after my
grandmother Jennie (Foley) Walsh. Her name was written in the Foley
family Bible as Mary Jannet Foley, yet she went by Jennie; Jennie is also
the name on her grave marker, a subject of confusion. I am not sure of
the source of Jennie, another family mystery I might never understand.
My late mother Margaret I. (Glieden) Walsh had a nickname of Peggy
to avoid confusion with her sister-in-law, Margaret A. Walsh, my aunt
and my father's sister. The confusion of the two Margarets continued
after my mother's death in 2011. Word incorrectly spread of my aunt's
death, rather than my mother's. There was yet more confusion the
following year, when a concerned local resident came to my house to
inquire if my aunt had died. I told my visitor I was on my way to visit
my Aunt Margaret in the nursing home in a few hours and was not
aware she had died, calling her on the phone to make sure, as I was her
guardian. Aunt Margaret did not die until 2013. I was with her when
she passed away in the middle of the night, as I had been staying in her
room along with my little dog for several days before her death. Bobby,
a Yorkshire terrier mixed-breed dog, was a surprise to the undertaker
in the middle of the night in my aunt's nursing home room. The two
Margarets are buried in the same family plot, separated by other family
members, clearly marking their relationships and dates of birth and
death, ending the lifetime of confusion.

It would not be a far stretch of the imagination for the rest of
family, including my ancestors, to think they lived ordinary lives,
maybe simple and poverty stricken at times, with no known royal
or aristocratic linages, depending on the state of their world in the
times they lived. My late mother, who lived most of her adult life in

Litchfield, Minnesota, once referred to her life as ordinary during one of our many discussions. But I truly do not believe this is an accurate description. She was born in rural Brooten, Minnesota, raised Catholic, with roots in Germany and Prussia. German was spoken at home, especially when her parents did not want the children to understand what was being said. Digging a bit deeper, there is a Lutheran branch of her family a few generations before my mother's birth. My mother spent seven years of her young adult life as a novice nun with the Franciscan Sisters of Little Falls, Minnesota.

Suffering came early for my mother. Her own mother died when she was seven; her father was unable to care for the family after their farm home was destroyed in a fire. My mother and her brothers and sisters went to live with other relatives during her childhood. She was essentially an orphan, but always retained her last name of Glieden. She survived the Great Depression of the 1930s, graduated from high school, and was brilliant in so many ways with her artistic abilities, always writing letters and reading books, magazines and just about anything she could. She gave birth to three children, mourned the death of one child, welcomed grandchildren into the world, and lived with chronic illnesses. She also enjoyed great joys during her life. My mother had an extraordinary life, not ordinary, surviving tremulous economic and political times, World War II, along with all of the rest that life brings.

I had just walked out of the judge's chambers in an Ocala, Florida, county courthouse in the early 2000s when a friend captured a photograph of me smiling like I had just been released from jail. There wasn't anything I had done wrong, but the photo just got it right. I was divorced and free to think and live my own life. The very first thing I needed to check on my divorce decree was that my maiden name was restored. At the county clerk's office, I skipped to the page indicating my name change. It was me again, with the name I was given at birth. I was Jannet Louise Walsh once again.

So, what's in my name? Starting with my first name, Jannet: it sounds like the popular French spelling of Jeannette. To break it down even more, it's pronounced Je-NET or Juh-NET. It's been a source of misspelling and bad pronunciation for as long as I can remember, all my life. My parents actually went to the source of a Foley family Bible to make sure Jannet was spelled correctly, the same as my grandmother's name, and were almost late to my baptism, as they wanted to make sure the spelling was correct. It was not until January 2019 that I was able to see photo copies of the Foley Bible my father made in the 1970s with the proof of the origin of my name.

Almost her entire life, my grandmother was called Jennie, with a grave marker engraved with Jennie, not Jannet. After Grandmother Jennie or Jannet's funeral, I tried to tell the old Irish Catholic priest, Father Thomas Diehl, that my grandmother's name was actually the same as mine, but he would hear nothing of it, almost starting a fight. I had to escape to the sanctuary of the kitchen with the women serving food and small glasses of red wine to guests at my grandparents' home.

The name Jannet has roots in Scotland, with the same meaning as the French version, Jeanette, the feminine form of John, which means "God is gracious." A few years ago, I found another source for the name in the Brittany region of France, frequented by Vikings, with deep Celtic heritage. This would be a great topic to explore more, and maybe there's a trip to Europe.

My grandmother Jennie's family comes from Luxembourg, a small country sandwiched between Germany and France. My great-grandmother Catherine Meier Foley was known for her French style of cooking, according to my Aunt Margaret.

One of my first jobs out of Ohio University after finishing my master of arts degree was at the *Omaha World-Herald*, as a staff photographer. I was always pleased to see my name under the photographs published in the newspaper, almost always spelled correctly. Often, I'd be greeted by the late editor, Gary Woodson "Woody" Howe, in the hallways at the paper, calling me Janet, sounding like JAN – et. I don't think I ever corrected the editor, as I was shy, or just afraid to correct him. I was later to understand he would send handwritten messages to other editors to make corrections on my name in the newspaper, to Janet. Messages apparently were passed back and forth for a while. If that twenty-something young woman could have only said something, the messages written in red ink likely would have stopped.

Today, I'm likely to stop anyone in their tracks from calling me Janet, and correct with this phrase: "My name is a trick name. It's Jannet, sounds like the French version, but it's never Janet."

If someone is rude and continues to call me the wrong name, I might start calling the offender by another name. Phone calls starting out by asking for Janet, are sometimes short when I say there is no person called Janet, unless I'm expecting a call related to a job offer, then I'll be happy to be called almost any name, including Janet.

My middle name is Louise, the first name of my maternal

grandmother, Louise Berger Glieden. Louise almost became my first name, according to my mother, but Jannet won out in first place. I wonder what life would have been like with a first name of Louise. Perhaps I'll just start using Louise; many people go by their second name.

Walsh, pronounced WALL-sh, is an Irish last name, with two syllables.

My name is so dear to me; it's who I am, but it also reflects my family and our past. My name is one of the best gifts my parents gave me. I'm using this gift each day.

Chapter 4

Shelbourne Hotel
Tea and Dad

June 4, 2018
Stauntons on the Green Hotel, St. Stephen's Green
Dublin, Ireland

I LISTEN TO THE SHARP SOUNDS OF A BLACK AND white bird, likely a magpie, resting outside my small hotel room for only a few moments, not long enough for me to take a photo. The hotel, Stautons on the Green,[2] located in the Georgian Quarter, is made up of three interlinked houses all built in 1750. Passing from one house to the next, the floors are not level. In the front of the building are white panels shielding the construction scaffolding as the houses are being restored.

Stauntons was home to famous residents. John Henry Newman, Catholic Cardinal, lived at Stauntons while he was busy founding the Catholic University of Ireland next door at Newman House. Henry Grattan, Irish politician had rooms here during the famous successful battle for Irish parliamentary independence. Business boomed in Ireland for two decades after his win in 1782. Poet Gerard Manley Hopkins lived his last years writing sonnets at his desk in this house. I was just lucky to find a room to lay my head down in busy Dublin while searching for my Irish family history.

There is a statue of Irish writer James Joyce, 1882–1941, near the entrance to St. Stephen's Green just opposite Newman University Church and Stauntons, helping to explain the meaning of the park, a public lawn for Dublin's city dwellers and visitors, strolling, dancing or relaxing. A quote by Joyce is inscribed on the statue; it begins, "Crossing Stephen's, that is my green..."

The location of Stauntons is precisely why I am staying here, along with a reasonably priced room. St. Stephen's Green, an entire

---

2.   https://www.stauntonsonthegreen.ie

Dublin city block, is just across the street, complete with band stands, fountains, walking paths, and a historic walking tour of the Easter Rising of 1916, a rebellion by Irish Republicans against British rule in Ireland. The Republicans sought an independent democratic republic in Ireland. Irish citizen-army volunteers occupied the park during the uprising. The Easter Rising was not a success, but an Irish Free State was declared in 1922.

Not far from Stauntons is the Shelbourne Hotel. Established in 1824, hotel guests were shot and injured while dining during the Easter Rising. This hotel is where my late father, Martin J. Walsh Jr., stayed in 1953.

Walking across the green to Shelbourne, I hear a family singing "In Dublin fair city, where the girls are so pretty . . . crying cockles and mussels, alive, alive oh."

I am sitting in the lobby of the Shelbourne waiting for my 11:30 am tea time in the Lord Mayor's Lounge. The historic drawing room takes its name from the date when the newly elected Mayors of Dublin celebrated their investiture in this very same lounge where I will have a classic afternoon tea, except in the late morning.

Precisely at 11:30 am, I am escorted to a table near the entrance with Wedgwood china and silverware. I select a flowering tea called Golden Fortune Balls, originating from China. The green leaf tea blossoms spin in front of me as hot water is poured into a glass teapot and piano music plays in a corner of the room. A yellow marigold flower occupies the middle of the tea ball, emitting a soft floral and slightly fruity scent. I place a large tea strainer over my teacup as I pour the tea.

Next, a tea tray with four stacked plates is delivered to my table with numerous little sandwiches, pastries, and other unfamiliar items. The bottom plate has house smoked salmon with mustard and pickled cucumber on Guinness bread; cherry tomato and St. Tola goat cheese on pumpkin bread; egg, mayonnaise, and watercress on white bread; and chicken and avocado on a poppy seed roll. All four tiny sandwiches roughly equal one typical American sandwich, yet they are truly elegant.

The Wedgwood china pattern matches the ceiling in this drawing room with a very ornate scrolled pattern. I'm told by the staff that the ceiling is original, making my view the same as my father might have had in 1953. An elegant Waterford crystal chandelier lights the room, and sunlight flows in from the large bay windows facing St. Stephen's

Green. I see yellow and red double decker buses passing by, while outlines of the same family singing about Dublin fair city enjoys their tea. Little girls wearing white flowing party dresses jump and dance between tables—afternoon tea at the Shelbourne, adding unexpected whimsey to the formal room.

According to hotel history, during the Easter Rising, afternoon tea was moved from the drawing room where I am now to where the Horseshoe Bar is now located in the lobby. The windows I look out were sandbagged and shuttered. The main entrance where I was greeted by a handsome doorman in a tall black hat and suit was barricaded, and wounded soldiers became guests during the Irish Civil War in 1922. I am sipping my tea on the spot of Ireland's battle for freedom. Today's visitors see the fine plates filled with tiny cheesecakes, chocolate and praline éclairs, but likely know little to nothing of the history of the room wrapped in Irish elegance, hospitality, and history.

After finishing my tea, I walk toward the guest reception and talk with Keith Geraghty, a concierge, asking for permission to look in the Shelbourne Museum for my father's registration. As I have a copy of a letter written by my father on May 13, 1953, on Shelbourne Hotel stationary, I should be able to quickly find his name in the records.

At first, I had difficulty locating the 1953 registration book, but soon held the large registry in my hands. Four inches thick, with a red and brown embossed cover, the name of the hotel in gold letters on the cover—it is an impressive object. I quickly go to May 1953 and start my search, quickly seeing my father's distinctive signature about halfway down page thirty-five.

Martin J. Walsh Jr., Murdock, Minnesota

The ledger indicates my father was scheduled to depart on May 14, 1953, staying in room 441, the sole occupant. Geraghty said that the numbering for the room has changed, and my father's room once looked over the Archbishop's house, which has been torn down to make room for government buildings, likely the Department of Agriculture, Food and the Marine located in current location, along with other buildings. In 1953, my father took a Victorian elevator to his floor, but the elevator was later removed.

Located just a few feet away from the old hotel registrars, including 1953 with my father's name, is a small wooden showcase with glass containing draft copies of the Irish Constitution from 1922, which were recovered by hotel staff from room 112, known as the Constitution Room. The chairman of the draft was Michael Collins, something like the American version of George Washington, helping to pave a path to a democratic Irish free state of home rule.

The Irish Constitution drafts from 1922 are difficult to read, the ink is fading, and there are splotches, handwritten corrections over the typed letters, and the glare from the lights on the glass covering makes concentration necessary if one is to read what helped change Ireland to a democracy.

Below is Article 1, page one of the 1922 Irish Constitution draft:

The Nations sovereignty extends not only to the men and women of the nation, but to all the material possessions of the nation, the Nation's soil and its resources and all the wealth and wealth-producing processes within the nation. All right to private property is subordinated to the public right and welfare of the nation. It is the duty of every man and woman to give allegiance and service to the commonwealth and it is the duty of the nation to ensure that every citizen shall have opportunity to spend his or her strength and faculties in the service of the people. In return for willing service it is the right of every citizen to receive and adequate share of the produce of the nation's labour.

While it had taken me just minutes to find my father's signature with the help of old letters from 1953 that I found at home in Murdock, Geraghty told me people search for hours. The following is one of the many letters my father sent home to his mother, Jennie Foley Walsh, during this 1953 trip with a stopover in Canada, followed by Ireland, and France. The Coronation my father writes about in 1953 was that of Queen Elizabeth II of the United Kingdom and other Commonwealth realms, June 2, 1953, London.

May 13, 1953
Airmail from Shelbourne Hotel, Dublin

Dear Mother,

I have been getting your letters okay. I took the train from Belfast to Dublin yesterday and I am at Dublin at presently. It is a very nice place and I am taking a tour today. It goes to Glendalough and Avoca and I am writing this on the bus while waiting for it to go out.

They have the most wonderful flowers in Dublin that I have ever seen. Peonies and tulips. I was at Mass today. I plan to stay here about a week and then to England and France. In England I may not stay hardly at all because the people are starting to come in for the Coronation and it makes rooms etc. hard to get. I am planning to go to Lourdes while in France.

It was nice Father Walsh was able to say Mass. The people over here are very friendly, and the weather has been quite good. Northern Ireland is making ready for the Coronation and they have flags and bunting, etc.

I have a pair of gloves for you, 2 pipes for Dad, a sweater for you, Agnes and Margaret. The train was very nice from Belfast to Dublin.

I am writing this during lunch hour on the tour I am on. The scenery etc. is simply grand. If you would write me Care of the American Express Company, Paris, France — I'll be able to get it okay. The South of Ireland is very nice as they don't have the British rule.

Tomorrow is the Holy Day, so I'll be attending Mass at Dublin. Our Bus driver on the tour is very interesting. And I know you would have liked him. I hope you are fine.

Cordially,
Martin

❧

Letter, May 23, 1953
Le Grand Hotel Du Louvre, Paris

In Paris, France, my father stayed at Le Grand Hotel Du Louvre according to his letter home to his mother. On May 23, 1953, he writes he's been in Paris for three days, and already toured the Palace of Versailles, and skips a trip to England.

"I flew down from Dublin on Wednesday as I wanted to bypass England as the coronation would make this too crowded. I could see England from the air, and it looks very nice."

My father had one chance in his life to visit England, but changed his travels due to preparations for Queen Elizabeth's coronation in 1953. I was delighted to read in his letters he viewed England, the island of Great Britain, from the air, flying from Dublin to Paris. He received an unexpected gift and memory he carried for a lifetime back home to Minnesota. I might call this the Queen's coronation gift to my father for a journey disturbed.

My father took a short trip to Lourdes, France, and bought a panoramic print of the city that still is displayed above the upright piano today at my home. He departed Le Harve, France, May 28, 1953, for New York City on the S. S. United States.

My father was born on December 7, 1924, in the house where I now live. I remember hearing the story as a child and always wondered how it could be as I thought babies are born only in hospitals. He was 17 on December 7, 1941, when Pearl Harbor was attacked. I was at my father's side when he died on December 6, 2008, in St. Luke's Hospital, in Duluth, Minnesota. A few days before his death, after he received the Sacrament of Last Rites, his final words to me were, "I love you."

Chapter 5

Civil War Solider
James G. Foley

June 21, 2018
Historic Washington County Courthouse
Stillwater, Minnesota

I READ THE WORDS PAINTED IN GOLD ABOVE THE VAULT door: Auditor, Washington Co., leading to the Vault Exhibit at the Historic Washington County Courthouse, built in 1886 in Stillwater, Minnesota. I study the old architectural plans drawn sometime before 1900, reported to be found wrapped around a wooden dowel and a sheet of oilcloth with a protective covering treated with tar or paint. Located next to the main entrance, the office of the County Auditor is clearly marked on the plans, just next to the vestibule in the corridor to the rotunda and double staircase of the old courtroom on the second floor. I walk to the office marked County Auditor on the old drawing, ask a few questions at the reception desk, only to find out the old drawing was recently placed in the Vault Exhibit room, so my timing was on track. I could not keep silent, and said I was now standing the same location, if the old plans are accurate, where James Gregory Foley served as Washington County Deputy Auditor for twenty years, and four years as Auditor, elected in 1880. James was born in Calais, Maine, March 15, 1843, the oldest child of William and Ellen Brennan Foley. I was now walking in the very location where an ancestor lived and breathed the same air, maybe better quality during his time, with a glimpse of the St. Croix River out of the corner office, if you look just right to the northeast. According to family history, flags on the Washington County House were lowered to half-staff in his honor at his death in 1914.

On January 22, 1862, at Fort Snelling, James enlisted in the Army at the age of nineteen for volunteer service for three years, with permission given to enlist by his father William Foley. During this time, he sent letters home from the battlefields of the Civil War, almost always addressed to his mother Ellen. Before war was declared, he acquired an education. James was engaged in lumbering in Stillwater, along with his father and the majority of the community. *The History of Washington County and the St. Croix Valley*, by Rev. Edward D. Neill, includes James as a pioneer in Washington County, with a short biography stating that James "participated in many of the leading battles. After the Battle of Vicksburg, he was prostrated by a sunstroke and conveyed to the hospital, and honorably discharged in 1865."

Neill's biography makes mention of James again embarking in lumbering after serving as a solider, but there is an alternative occupation known to my family. After the Civil War, he spent six years in California and Nevada prospecting for gold, returning to marry Miss Elizabeth A. Colsen in 1877. They had eight children.

In 1991, my relatives Ed and Colleen Foley discovered five letters written by James to his mother at the National Archives in Washington DC. On November 10, 1896, a letter was written to D. J. Murphy, Federal Commissioner of Pensions, to document James's service and receive a pension for his military service with Company K Regiment, Minnesota Volunteers, during the Civil War. In the last line of the letter, James asks that the old letters not be thrown in the wastebasket, but kindly returned to him. Although only five letters were received by Murphy, there were perhaps one hundred letters available for inspection, but it is unknown where the other letters are today.

The first in the series of letters by James is one of the most dramatic, giving a description of the First Battle of Corinth on May 28, 1862. He slept with no blanket for several weeks. Below is the complete letter, originally handwritten, but transcribed by Ed and Colleen Foley, as it is difficult to read some of the handwriting. Letters have a stamp from the Pensions Office received November 14, 1896, and also a stamp from the National Archives. The first letter, and the other four letters by James, are the closest I will likely ever come to understanding my Irish ancestors, or any family after immigration to the United States. I do not know the outcome of the request for the pension, but what is more valuable are the letters now living on for future generations preserved by the National Archives.

Letter One: No Blanket after Battle of Corinth

March 21, 1863
Camp near Helena, Arkansas

Dear Mother, I take my pen in hand to write you these few lines, hoping to find you enjoying as good health as this leaves me in at present. Thank God for all his mercies to us undeserving mortals.

I went out across the slough to the main land this afternoon and culled a few May flowers of apple blossoms and some lilacs. I will send them in this letter to you and Mary and Ella, so that you can say you had May flowers before any of the little girls around.

The weather is very hot here. The sun pours down in the middle of the day and cools off toward evening.

Dear Parents, you must not fret after me. I will return to you after the war happy and victorious and will have gained a great deal of experience in the short term of three years. I will live content at home. With your leave, I will continue my story, next page.

I will tell you about my first Battle of Corinth, in Mississippi, May 28, 1862, sleeping without my blanket for many days.

In the evening, they [Confederates] commenced to shell us again with cannons.

That day we had nothing to eat nor in the evening except what we had in our haversacks. That night we were ordered to dig entrenchments for the 11th Missouri right on our left and we dug all night, imagine our feelings, if you can.

About midnight I got tired and fell asleep on the side of a grave newly made. The ground was softer in that spot than anywhere else. I was awakened about two o'clock and went to work again.

We were very hungry, indeed, and two or three of us went off begging to another regiment and seeing some meat and hard bread cooking we told them that we had had nothing to eat for two days. After they were done, they invited us to eat. And we did eat, I tell you.

General Pike was laying asleep under the shade of a tree near where we were placed. He did not seem to mind it at all.
That night we all went to sleep expecting to have a hard time next day, as our general rode around telling the men that they would be in Corinth next night or in hell. All that night we could hear the cars whistling and the drums beating in Corinth very distinctly. They were evacuating. [Union General]

About 9 o'clock am on the 30th, we received the news that Corinth was evacuated, and those sounds we had heard were magazines blowing up all the railcars.

We marched west from the battlefield and took the road toward Clear Creek. We marched until 9 o'clock pm. We were all very much fatigued and we lay down to sleep. I did not have any blanket, but my overcoat.

Our cavalry took about 500 prisoners. General Pike magnified it to 5,000, but the truth came out afterward and it was found out that we took but 500. We remained at this place (Clear Creek) about a week, when one hot morning we were ordered to march.

We did not have much packing to do, as we had no tents at this time and I had no blanket, but still my backpack was excessively heavy having many things which were unnecessary in it. We marched twenty miles. I will not dwell on the thousand and one little incidents on the road, but merely the principal things which happened.

Each man had to carry about 40 lbs. at the least, calculated. I put your white handkerchief over my head (or cap) and tied the corners in my mouth. I could not breath any other way for the dust was so thick that you could not see a man two feet off.

In the evening, the men began to fall down, some died, and some were sick for months afterward and some never recovered the effects of that march. 50 men in our regiment was all that arrived at Clear Creek. Next night, I was one of them. I lay down under a tree and I was very stiff and sore and all blisters on my feet.

Your son,
James G. Foley

Chapter 6

Grandpa Martin

April 30, 2022
Murdock, Minnesota

IN THE LIVING ROOM. I'M PULLING A LARGE STUFFED
arm chair way from the south wall, situated to the right of the
upright piano in the corner. There's always been two stuffed chairs next
to the piano long as I remember. I'm not in the process of rearranging
furniture, but need to take the large portrait of my grandfather Martin J.
Walsh Sr. (1887–1988) off the wall. I need to get a better look at Grandpa
Martin.

I carry the large, framed color portrait out to the newest part of the
house built in 2019 and finished in 2020 during the pandemic. This
room is built over old foundation walls of the flour mill discovered
during construction. I'm not sure where to place the large 11 by 14 inch
photographic portrait.

With little thought at all, I place Grandpa's portrait on a large
stuffed chair next to me where I'm seated at my computer with stacks
of notebooks and family research. It just seems like the natural thing
to do—sit next to Grandpa. He's about ninety-four years old in this
photograph. Grandpa had a twin sister, but she died at birth. There
are few details, and her name is not known. This fact was revealed by
Aunt Margaret in 1991.

The photo was taken by my brother Paul M. Walsh about 1980,
as student at St. Cloud State University. The camera Paul used was a
vintage 1940s or 1950s Rollei Twin Lens Reflex, 2¼ x 2¼ inch, medium
format camera, creating a good sized negative for enlargements, just
like the very photograph in front of me. About 1972, Paul, age ten
or eleven, photographed the late Hubert H. Humphrey, then United
States Senator from Minnesota, at the county fair in Litchfield,
Minnesota. Paul wrote Humphrey and received a reply back with
an autographed photograph asking him if he was going to become a
photographer when he grows up. Our father told Paul not to show the
photo of Humphrey to Grandpa as it would upset him. Paul remembers
a similar reaction by Grandpa when Humphrey flew into the Murdock

Municipal, likely the Murdock Centennial Parade, 1978. Grandpa's ill feelings were likely related to Humphrey's support for the Vietnam War as Vice President, under President Lyndon B. Johnson, but it is hard to know why Grandpa was upset about Humphrey. Paul went on to have a successful career as a newspaper photojournalist and TV photographer.

What I see before me is Grandpa smiling in this portrait, seated with his back to the east, and the piano at his left shoulder. He is sitting is one of his favorite chairs in the living room. He has no hair, but as a young man on his wedding day he had more than enough red hair. It's a little hard to make out his eyeglasses, but the temple and bridge appear to be a horn-rimmed color. I see reflections from the reading lights or photographic lights on the eyeglass lenses. This photo gives me a good look into my grandpa's eyes, looking to be green in color.

Grandpa is wearing a white Oxford style shirt buttoned to the top, with a magenta-colored tie and diagonal blue stripes with a Windsor knot, or maybe it's a pretied Windsor knot clip on style tie. His cardigan sweater is buttoned, except for the top button. His right hand is placed over his left hand, and part of his wristwatch is peeking out from the cuff of his left sleeve. With this information, wearing his watch on his left arm, he's likely right-handed. Legs are crossed, left over right leg, wearing dark colored trousers, seated on a stuffed brown armchair, with dark polished wood on the hand rests. In the background I can see the old white damask curtains, and there is a gold-colored cloth covering the headrest and back of the chair.

What remains today from this four-decade old photo is the chair, since recovered by my aunt Margaret with a floral design sometime in the 1980s or later. The location of the chair today is just a few feet away from the day my Grandpa's photograph was made by Paul. The piano is still located in the corner, likely needing to be tuned again, although it was tuned twice sometime after 2010.

Looking at the portrait of Grandpa, I have an urge to visit the cemetery, and it's just a few minutes after noon. I hitch the leash to my dachshund's harness, tuck a notebook and pen under my raincoat, and walk briskly in the drizzling rain, now about 52 degrees.

It's the first visit to Sacred Heart Cemetery in 2022, and want to pray at my family's graves. Looking west at these graves, it's Aunt Margaret, Grandpa, Grandma, my baby brother David, my father, and my mother.

After a quick prayer I think how lucky my brother and I both worked at collecting family stories from Grandpa when he was in his nineties. Looking at the six graves of my family before me, I know there are many stories lost in time, buried forever beneath me. We are lucky to have collected as many details as possible from Grandpa.

ᨄ

As students at St. Cloud State University, Paul and I both collected stories from Grandpa for history courses, especially for an American Studies 101 course called Family American-Life, taught by now Professor Emeritus William T. Morgan in 1983. If I recall correctly, we were taking the same course, but at different times during the winter quarter. It was my second quarter as a college student, and my transcript reports I earned letter grade of A. No matter the grade I earned, it's the stories from Grandpa that's most important from the academic year of 1982 to 1983, not reflected in my college transcripts. As a freshman, Paul also wrote about Grandpa for a Minnesota History course with the late Professor Emeritus Calvin W. Gower. Knowing our family history was so valuable, he revised and improved on Grandpa's stories in 1983.

Looking at my brother's 1983 term paper from St. Cloud State, he mentions Grandpa recently suffered a severe stroke in 1983 or perhaps earlier. Grandpa is still living at home, but no longer recalls many of his past events mentioned in his term paper. In other words, Paul was very lucky to capture Grandpa's stories before it was too late.

Paul shared with me he wrote down the entire interview of Grandpa at home in Murdock, not using a tape recorder. Of course, I wanted to know if it was in the living room, or in the kitchen Paul interviewed Grandpa, but he was not sure. The chances are very high, Grandpa was sitting in the chair featured in his photograph.

I have a memory from winter 1983, interviewing Grandpa in the living room, and Aunt Margaret sat next to me on the sofa, and Grandpa in his chair. Grandpa had difficulties talking due to his stroke. Aunt Margaret, Paul, along with my parents, helped put together my term paper, along with details I was able to receive directly from Grandpa.

Clearly this shows the time to collect family stories is now, as priceless heritage can be lost in a blink of an eye, or in this case for my family, a stroke. It is also fortunate Sister Julitta Walsh also interviewed Grandpa in 1976, providing another source for family history, although many of the stories area repeated, but also very helpful.

❧

Digging into Paul's paper, "A Century of Stories of the Walsh Family," dated February 21, 1983, the first thing that's noticeable is this paper was typed on a typewriter. Paul doesn't recall the make or model, not an IBM, but it was an electric typewriter, making every single letter a chore, and barely worked. When he typed too fast, the letters jammed, and the typebar, or strikers, would often collide. There are a few places where corrections were made with a liquid whiteout, all typical of this period for college papers. Paul starts out in the opening paragraphs by mentioning our family's limited history.

"Many of the early stories and history of the Walsh family are limited and have been lost and forgotten through the years. But many of these stories are still alive and seem as if they were only historical events from yesterday when you talk to my grandfather Martin J. Walsh Sr. He can recall dates, events, and especially political events, as well as today's current events."

Paul writes it was common on many Sunday afternoons, almost anyone enjoyed listening to Grandpa for hours telling stories, giving color to his stories like no other person he knew. Grandpa's friends and family would stop to visit, coming for the storytelling, as it was common practice in his day. Most of Paul's interview is written in first person from Grandpa, adding a more personal delivery of stories beyond his diary entries.

In Grandpa's own words, "I was baptized on Holy Thursday, 1887, at St. Bridget's Catholic Church in De Graff, and confirmed in April 1899, by Bishop James Trobec." The baptism record of Grandpa's day is as significant as a birth certificate is today.

In my interviews with Grandpa, as for Paul, it was important for Grandpa to say he was born in Section 32 in Dublin Township, in Swift County, in a house moved out from De Graff by his grandfather Michael Walsh Sr. I would stumble when Grandpa referenced a section of the township instead of street address. I understand now that a section of land is about one square mile, and there are thirty-six sections in a township. The house Grandpa mentions was, at his birth, a shanty house used by early settlers.

✌

Grandpa Martin's only formal education was grade school in Dublin Township. He went to school in District 32, originally known as the Lafthus School after Thomas Lafthus, located in Section 26 of Dublin Township. District 32 was organized in 1878, and Lafthus and others petitioned for a school to be built.

The old school was sold to Pete Cain, and in 1902, a new school was built one half mile south of the old school on land owned by Patrick McGinty. Grandpa mentions enrollment was between fifty and sixty students, and attendance exceeded seating capacity. For some time, the school operated on split shifts, with half the students coming in the morning, and half in the afternoon.

According to Swift County history, School District 32, still located in Section 26 of Dublin Township, hired Mart Walsh as the first janitor of the new building at the rate of 10 cents a day, 1903. Mart is my Grandpa, his nickname. The job as janitor might be one of his first paid jobs. He was about sixteen years of age, and his formal education was likely completed, not going to high school or other formal education, instead helping his family on the farm.

According to my brother's interview, Grandpa was a leader behind a rebellion in the schoolhouse of District 32. "I can remember many of the early teachers and their names very well. Miss Mills was probably the best qualified teacher with a good certificate." Grandpa mentions another teacher not as qualified. One day the not-so-qualified male teacher accused Grandpa's brother Henry Walsh with some misdemeanor and pointed at him to leave the schoolhouse.

"So, I rose in Henry's defense, and tried to reason with him, to no avail. Then I announced to the class, 'Well, we may as well all go home.'" All but a few students remained in the classroom. As a result of the rebellion, the teacher was removed, and replaced by Miss Mills.

This is not the first time I've heard about the schoolhouse rebellion, and Paul's version adds more details about the situation. This shows Grandpa's strong character at a young age, seeing right from wrong, and taking action. Grandpa was lucky to stand up for his brother Henry in the schoolhouse that day. Later in life, Henry would stand up as best man at Grandpa's wedding, and they would live in homes side by side until nearly the end of their lives in Murdock.

❦

Grandpa says baseball was very popular with the Walsh family during his discussion with Paul. There was a local baseball team called the Dublin Colts that started about 1900. Grandpa's oldest brother Michael Francis Walsh, known as Francis, played on few ball teams.

It was common knowledge Grandpa loved baseball. Many visits as a child to Murdock I'd find Grandpa listening to his portable radio, Zenith Royal 710, about the size of a lunch box or another portable transistor radio about the size of a hand. He would be tuned to WCCO radio station or other stations broadcasting the Minnesota Twins games, including late into the night, resting in his bed. Daily agendas for Grandpa were set around when the Twins games were broadcasted. Aunt Margaret would announce upon arrival to Murdock if Grandpa had a game on for the day, meaning he was listening to the Twins during the visit. Although Grandpa had new transistor radios, he would still listen to an old wooden radio that had AM, and also shortwave. There used to be a long wire that would go out the window and attach to a tree so Grandpa could listen to shortwave radio stations.

❦

The Great Hinckley Fire of 1894, located near Hinckley, Minnesota, started September 1, burning three hundred fifty thousand acres or more, about four hundred square miles. There were at least 418 men, women, and children who lost their lives during the fire. Countless animals, livestock, and wildlife were also lost. At this time there was a steady loss of moisture in central Minnesota, reported from 1891 to 1894 by the St. Paul Weather Bureau.

My Grandpa was about seven years old at the time of the Hinckley Fire, living with his family in rural Dublin Township. Hinckley is about one hundred fifty miles northeast of rural Dublin Township in Swift County. Grandpa shares his memories of the fire: "I remember the Hinckley fire. On September 1, 1894, a neighbor had come over to our farm near Murdock to borrow a wagon during the harvest. When we went outside, the smoke was so thick in the air from the fire up north that their eyes just burned from the smoke." The farm Grandpa is likely talking about in Dublin Township was located not far from the Chippewa County line.

In 1987, while writing a story about my Grandpa's one-hundredth birthday for the West Central Tribune, the Willmar newspaper, I wrote about the smoke from the Hinckley fire. The editor at that time said that it just wasn't possible for the smoke to come all the way to Murdock, removing sentences I wrote about the smoke. I remember mentioning more than once the facts about the fire, and what Grandpa said. The editor shook his head in disbelief, yet published my story.

July 29, 2021, the skies and air in Murdock were filled with smoke far away as Canada. My house and yard were surrounded in a haze of orange and yellow smoke from Canadian forest fires, needing to wear a face mask to go outside. I have no doubts of the story Grandpa shared about the Great Hinckley fire as I've experienced firsthand smoke from fires in Canada, much farther away than Hinckley.

❧

Grandpa shares more details about village and rural life, growing up in Dublin Township. "Back then there were no such things as mail route or country telephones. And the main source of entrainment were the country dances at the Town Hall. The Murphys, especially Billy Murphy, the harness maker, and his brother Walter were the main musicians," said Grandpa.

It's unknown if Grandpa is referring to dances in De Graff, Murdock, Kerkhoven or Benson, but it sure it's certain he was intrigued by dancing at about age fourteen. "The two-step started at the turn of the century. In fact, I first saw it danced at the Minnesota State Fair in 1901 when I went with my father. Waltzing and square dancing were always popular." The two-step has a pattern of two quick steps followed by two slow steps.

❧

Grandpa's first encounter with Teddy Roosevelt happens the same year at the state fair when he sees the two-step dance. He sees then Vice President Theodore Roosevelt give a speech about foreign policy at the fairgrounds, hearing some very famous words said, September 2, 1901, St. Paul, Minn.

"It was at the fair in 1901 when I heard Teddy Roosevelt make the famous statement, 'Speak softly and carry a big stick.'"

There were about ten thousand people at the grandstand for the opening fair address. The Minnesota state fair is credited as the first public use of this famous saying. It was about two weeks later after the Minnesota "big stick" speech when Roosevelt was sworn in as president after the assassination of President William McKinley.

❧

Grandpa as a young man, about age twenty, worked hard during harvest season keeping a steam powered engine tractor or a steam traction engine operating. The engine, connected with a long belt, was used to power a threshing machine for the purpose of removing seeds from stalks and husks. The fuel used to boil water in the steam engine ranged from coal, oil, and straw.

Grandpa describes his job, likely called a fireman, although he does not call it that. "In 1907 I fired an engine in Michigan and North Dakota all fall. There were fourteen bundle teams with two tank wagons hauling water. I earned a top salary of $3.50 a day. Most worked for $1.00 or $1.25 at this time. They burned macaroni wheat straw at first and later switched to flax straw which worked better. At two different occasions, they were forced to shut down to clean the boiler, as the steam engine was foaming because of the alkali in the poor water."

❧

Grandpa told Paul a story about a blizzard and his serious illness in 1909, about age twenty-two. "On January 31, 1909, was a one-day blizzard. My brother Francis was building his barn which was blown off its foundations. There were very high winds and heavy snow, but mild weather, certainly an unusual blizzard for Minnesota. In the fall of this same year, I was treated for Typhoid Fever by Dr. Hans Johnson from Kerkhoven. At this time, he visited his patients on motorcycle. I was sick for about four weeks. My drug bill at Stroms in Benson was higher than the doctor's bill. As a result of this illness, I missed the wedding of Francis Walsh and Julia (Longman) on October 20, 1909. Dr. Johnson said that I had contracted the fever at the State Fair from contaminated water."

Stroms Drug store was located in Benson on Pacific Avenue between 13th and 14th Streets, and was in business from about 1896 to 1924, according to Swift County Historical Society.

Also in 1909, on the way to the Minnesota State Fair, Grandpa mentions he traveled on the train from Murdock with old John Smith. Smith insisted they get off at the station in Wayzata, stay over at his home, a place called Victoria, and go to the fair from there. It's hard for me to think Grandpa was traveling with just old John Smith, but likely he was with his brother Henry or another brother.

⚉

Fast forward to Willmar, Minnesota, Sunday, September 4, 1910, Grandpa is about twenty-three, standing in the crowd gathered of an estimated three to six thousand people at the Willmar train station to see and listen to then former President Roosevelt during a whistle stop tour.

Before me now, I have an enlarged postcard of the image of Col. Theodore Roosevelt by E. Elkjar, a prominent Willmar photographer in the 1910s. Roosevelt is standing and speaking from the back of a railroad car, as depicted in my enlarged photograph. This same image is part of the Library of Congress photograph collection.

It would be great if I could find my young Grandpa in this photo in the crowd of thousands surrounding the train with Roosevelt, but that's just not possible. I can see the backs of men and women, almost all wearing hats, along with a few children lifted or riding on the shoulders of adults. I am seeing gentlemen wearing fat-topped straw boater hats with wide ribbons around their crowns.

I have memories of dilapidated and old straw flat hats with the tops popped out, and brims separated from the crowns like the ones in the 1910 photograph. Grandpa's old boater hats and winter overboots were once stored in the front entry closet at home in Murdock when I was a child. Aunt Margaret cleared them out many years ago.

With the help of the Willmar Tribune, Aug. 31, 1910, announcing Roosevelt's visit, I am able to find out a few details about the train car in the photograph. A special train was expected to arrive between noon and 12:30 pm, September 4, 1910, at the Willmar train station, consisting of an engine, baggage car and two Pullman, sleeping cars, called the Forest and Republic. It's likely Roosevelt is standing on the back section of a Pullman, the Forest or Republic.

The train departed earlier in the morning on September 4 from Sioux Falls, and was expected to take four hours to travel about 138 miles before arriving in Willmar. From Willmar, and after changing train crews and inspections, the train was heading to Fargo for another engagement the following day, September 5.

After arriving in Willmar, Roosevelt's train was greeted with patriotic national colors and his last name in large letters. The news story reports the railroad tracks were lined with autos nearby, and surrounding streets.

As Fargo was the next stop for Roosevelt, west of Willmar, and the train was pointing east, the crowd needed to wait for the train to be turned around using the "Y," or wye, located near the station. A wye track is an arrangement of railroad tracks in the form of the letter "Y" used for turning engines, and rail cars. It's something like a three-point turn using railroad tracks shaped like a triangle on a grand scale.

Roosevelt apparently reported he was not going to make any speeches in Willmar as he wanted to rest since it was Sunday, instead calling it a sermon, he spoke about citizenship, its duties and responsibilities, and a few more topics.

There is one quote that stands out for me from Roosevelt's Willmar visit in 1910, as perhaps did of the women of that day. Roosevelt talked about overworked housewives needing to be given more consideration. "I have little use for a man who will buy all the latest improved machinery and implements for doing his work on the farm and will deny his overworked wife those conveniences which she needs to lessen the drudgery of her work," stated Roosevelt.

My grandfather was not yet married when he heard this message, and hope he was listening. He must have been listening as my grandmother Jennie had modern conveniences in the kitchen and loved to host parties.

Before Roosevelt departs Willmar, he is given a bouquet of long-stemmed asters by a young girl, and he waves to the crowd while thanking them for their attention as the "train glided away over the glistening rails," writes the Willmar Tribune, September 7, 1910.

꧁꧂

The same year Grandpa sees Teddy Roosevelt in Willmar, he starts a new job. "In the fall of 1910, I started to work with the Page Fence Company as a traveling collector. Later I worked for the Adrian Wire Company. I worked mostly in Minnesota, but my biggest sales were in South Dakota."

Grandpa Martin, about age twenty-eight, and Grandma Jennie, about age twenty-nine, marry Nov. 4, 1915. Two years later, June 5, 1917, Grandpa, now age thirty, registers for the World War I draft for military service. He claims an exemption from the draft on the grounds of dependent relatives. The dependents listed are wife and child; my Grandma and Aunt Agnes, all still living at the hotel in Murdock.

A few interesting facts listed in Grandpa's draft registration include he is a traveling salesman working on commission, married, and race is Caucasian. His physical appearance is listed as tall, medium built, brown hair, and gray eyes.

My memory suggests his eyes were green. Grandpa's eyes look green in his large portrait I have before me. Paul remembers Grandpa saying his hair was red. I was told by my mother Grandpa's hair was red also. This is a good case to not relying on documents to collect family history, but instead collect as many details and stories directly from family.

⚜

In 1922, when my grandparents moved into their new Murphy house in Murdock, Grandpa began working for International Harvester, on October 2 or 3. Grandpa traveled a lot for his work. "I was a traveling collector who had the responsibility of collecting payments and repossessing machinery. I considered myself lucky, because during the depression jobs were hard to find. I stopped working for International Harvester at the time of Pearl Harbor in 1941."

At home in Murdock, Martin J. Walsh Jr., celebrated his seventeenth birthday on December 7, 1941, Pearl Harbor Day. Dad registered for the draft on December 28, 1942, age eighteen, as a student at St. Thomas College, St. Paul. He was enlisted in the army during World War II for one day, and discharged the same day, spending a career working for the railroad.

Regarding repossessing farm implements, my brother Paul in the early 1980s encountered someone or a family member of someone who had a tractor or other machinery repossessed near Murdock. The chances are high they were even related to Grandpa given the small rural community.

Today, I'd like to make it very clear it was the company, International Harvester, not my Grandpa, who was owed money for the farm machinery. Grandpa was doing his job, and needed to care for his wife and children. This is a bit of history that's still difficult today to understand, combined with the struggles of the Great Depression. Grandpa did not go without difficulties during this time.

⚜

Grandpa shares some of his difficulties during the agricultural depression. "During the depression farming was very bad. In 1934 there were no crops, and the banks closed. I lost money in the bank stock. But I was lucky, because some of the people got cleaned out. The Kerkhoven bank opened after it was allowed to reopen. The price of land was now very low. Much of the land sold for $25 or less an acre. In 1934 wheat was 43 cents a bushel in Minneapolis, but 1934, there was a crop failure. In 1935 the crop situation was so bad that farmers had to import seeds for crops."

Having one job was not enough to survive during Grandpa's day, as is the reality in 2022. Grandpa was also selling newspaper subscriptions. "I was also working with the Minneapolis Star since 1938. . . . I sold on commission until 1948, when I was forced to work directly for the company. I retired in June 1952, qualifying for maximum Social Security with pension from the Star and Tribune." The newspaper was later named Star Tribune.

⚜

In about 1983 Grandpa Martin was about ninety-five years of age when he was interviewed by Paul. Grandma Jennie was about ninety-six. "The dollar won't buy as much as it used to, but I am living very comfortably in good health with my wife, Jennie. My favorite pastime is playing cards and listening to ball games. God has truly blessed me throughout my life."

In the late 1970s or early 1980s, one day I went looking for Grandpa downtown Murdock playing cards with his friends at the bar. It's very unlikely he was drinking alcohol, but I can't say for sure. I remember finding Grandpa sitting with other old men playing cards. I was excited to see him, but he was very focused on his card playing. He didn't think I should be in the bar, telling more than once to leave and go back home. Reluctantly, and confused, I walked back home.

⚜

Paul mentions that during the early 1980s, Murdock appears different, with a consolidated school district. The Murdock school combined with surrounding communities of nearby Sunburg and Kerkhoven. There are many businesses in Murdock that have closed, or since torn down their buildings. The old Great North Railway Depot was still being used as a repair shop at the time of Paul's interview with Grandpa, but the train station has since been removed.

"But there is still that feeling of a small town when you can go to the grocery store and charge your groceries and everyplace is within a fifteen-minute walk," writes Paul. Lang's Grocery and McGovern's Grocery were two of the last grocery stores in Murdock, both gone now for decades. The nearest grocery stores are in Benson and Willmar, or the combined general store and hardware in Kerkhoven. Paul said our dad worked at one of the stores in Murdock when he was young, stocking shelves with merchandise. It's likely where he learned about collecting coins, including a 1916 rare Mercury dime.

⚜

Paul writes about our grandparent's old house, now my home. "The old house was a place of activities and functions. It was a place grandmother's brother Mike Foley would stop on his way to town and would do his laundry. During the summer for about six weeks, it was home to nuns who would teach Catechism. The yard was a place to put the big tent for all the neighboring kids to play in." Remains of the old canvas tent was found in the attic about 2010.

During the time of the 1920s and 1930s, there was no such thing as kindergarten in Murdock for children. Grandpa mentions school would start at the age parents sent their children to school. The first three years students were all together, and home room had things like art. It was common for students to walk home for lunch during the school day, smelling freshly baked bread.

Paul writes, "There were always ways you could get into trouble even in a small town after school. While in the third or fourth grade, my aunts (Agnes and Margaret) took an expedition into the country and got lost. It took many people to look for them."

⚜

Grandpa said most of the activities in Murdock took place at home or with the church. "There were sometimes trips with the church. It was always fun to listen to the records on the wind-up record player, make candy and homemade ice cream, or quilt making with a lot of people. Sometimes the bridge club would have meetings in the house." There were apparently movies in Murdock, according to Grandpa, the big event of the week. One of his friends would play the piano for the background music, meaning the movies were silent, didn't have sound.

Grandpa was away from home a great deal, seldom at home for his jobs. Many duties of raising three children were left to Grandma Jennie at home, yet she was very busy with activities. Grandma kept a very prominent position in local church society, taking care of the altar at the Catholic church in Murdock, along as being a good organizer for the Red Cross, and working as a seamstress, often sewing wedding dresses for area ladies. It's known Grandma Jennie went to a sewing or finishing school in Stillwater, Minnesota, as a young woman before she married. Her sewing brought in additional income for the family, and kept her busy while Grandpa was away from the house working. Grandma's Singer sewing machine was made in early 1928 and likely purchased just before the Stock Market Crash of 1929 and the Great Depression.

∼❧∽

On or about February 19, 1987, Grandpa Martin celebrated with a birthday party at home in Murdock, including his friend Father Thomas Diehl, 1930–1988, of Sacred Heart in Murdock. Aunt Margaret went all out, inviting guests to congratulate Grandpa on his one-hundredth birthday. I can see him is the living room, seated in a wheelchair, with a wool blanket draped over his shoulders, wearing a red and white flower pinned to his sweater, left shoulder. He's smiling, and laughing, as he's greeted by friends and family bringing him cards, now piling up on his lap. He could barely talk now, but could smile, and one could see he was happy. Paul asked Grandpa on his birthday what it was like to be 100. Grandpa replied he was just too old!

Paul was busy taking photographs of the party and of Grandpa, the birthday boy. My mother and Aunt Margaret were in the kitchen preparing food, along with other ladies. I doubt if all 100 candles were used on the birthday cake. It's an incredible achievement to live for one century. Grandma Jennie was already gone, died in 1985, age ninety-eight.

∼❧∽

Upstairs are calendars from the last years of Grandpa's life tucked away in the closet in his bedroom. Each day was marked with an "X", or with the names of the visitors added for the day, including when the parish priest brought by Holy Communion, or just paid Grandpa a visit.

Grandpa Martin's heart fails after more than one hundred years of life; dies at 4:54 pm, Friday, January 15, 1988, at Rice Memorial Hospital, Willmar. My father, Martin J. Walsh Jr., and Aunt Margaret were with Grandpa when he died. He's just short of age 101, with his birthday day of February 19.

I remember making a quick decision to fly home from my first job working at a newspaper in Beatrice, Nebraska, working as a photojournalist. My father picked me up from the airport in Minneapolis, and we drove home. Paul was at graduate school for photography at Ohio University, in Athens, Ohio, making it difficult to travel home quickly. The funeral was January 18, 1988, just three days after Grandpa's death.

I can't remember details of the actual funeral, but I do remember the night before at Sacred Heart Catholic Church. Grandpa's coffin is open before a prayer or rosary service. I talk with Jack Clarke, one of Grandpa's old and dearest friends, living across from the Catholic church in Murdock. The very place of Grandpa's coffin is where the two friends would exchange magazines and newspapers for years after Mass. Mr. Clarke, as Aunt Margaret always called him, was crying. I was crying. Mr. Clarke had the *Newsweek* magazine subscription, and Grandpa, *Time* magazine. Paul wanted to keep a 1979 issue of *Time* featuring Ansel Adams, but this messed up the exchange system with Mr. Clark and Grandpa. Paul still has the copy today.

The day of the funeral I vaguely recall in the church walking behind Grandpa's coffin, standing near my parents and aunts, but no other memories of the funeral in the church.

I remember standing near the open grave at Sacred Heart Catholic Cemetery. Mr. Clarke was of the active casket bearers, helping to place Grandpa Martin to rest. Five other men, Henry Walsh, James Walsh, Joseph Foley, Leo Laughlin, and Walter Walsh, were all there to help Grandpa for the last time, sending him on his journey home.

❧

Grandpa's photograph briefly brought him back to life for me today. It's now time to place the portrait of Grandpa on the next to Grandma in the living room, just next to the piano.

As grandchildren, Paul and I will likely remember Grandpa as playfulness when we were young. "Grandpa used to put coins under the seat cushion for us every time we would come to the house to visit. This came from the time I found coins under the cushion, and then after that Grandpa would put coins for us to find during our visits," said Paul.

Chapter 7

Murdock on the Edge of the World

A COPY OF A BLACK AND WHITE TINTYPE PHOTOGRAPH, circa 1862, of my great-granduncle James, likely at nineteen when he enlisted in the US Army, dressed in his Civil War uniform, posing with three of his brothers, including my great-grandfather Stephen Foley, gives a glimpse of the young solider. A copy of the tintype was kept in my grandmother Jennie's bedroom. She could identify personally the people in the photograph, while I must rely on documentation associated with the image as I am three generations removed. Wishing I could have a conversation with my grandmother Jennie about the weather or this year's crops from the family farm is all I can do.

While James stayed in Stillwater to live out his life after returning home to Minnesota after the Civil War, his brother Stephen Foley, my great-grandfather along with my pioneering Walsh family, arrived from Ireland and Canada, and other locations, firmly establishing foundations in rural Swift County, Minnesota.

Many sunrises and sunsets have passed since my family arrived in Swift County, yet I continue to see farmland and landscapes with churches and grain elevators marking the skyline of Murdock, Minnesota, all located very close to the edge of the world.

Murdock Skyline Looking East

Details are from my watercolor sketch, June 6, 2015

All buried in the cemetery have their feet pointing east. Look for the large Irish Celtic crosses, and find the priests, Father Walsh with his Irish walking stick, looks west, all ready for the Second Coming of Christ.

A stand of trees surrounds the outermost boundary, with railroad cars passing by homes and businesses.

Tiny corn grows on the edge of Murdock.

Bell tower of the Catholic Church stands proud.

Chimes sound at the top and bottom of the hour.

The water tower peeks out just above the tree line, best viewed looking north from the US Post Office.

The grain elevator is the skyscraper. Crops sold and sent out west by rail, then on to Asia.

Hidden from a stand of trees is home, just one house from the cemetery.

The skyline view looking east of Murdock is complete.

Little is changing. Absolutely perfect view.

October 14, 2018
Murphy House Walsh Family Home
Murdock, Minnesota

Actor Buster Keaton was busy in Hollywood making silent movies in 1922, but my family was making their own history in rural Swift County in Minnesota, specifically Dublin Township, in the village of Murdock. If only a movie crew had arrived in rural Minnesota to create a silent movie of my grandparents on their wedding day, November 4, 1915, at Sacred Heart Catholic Church in Murdock, and the day they moved into their first and only house.

I will have to guess my grandparents had a Ford automobile, likely a Model T, as the Model T had been out for several years. Their Ford would be parked next to be curb or on the driveway next to the house as my grandparents, Martin J. Walsh Sr. and Jennie Foley Walsh, started moving their household goods to their new home on September 16, 1922, known as the Murphy House, after the builders and first owners of the house on Main Avenue. They spent their first night in their house two days later, September 18, 1922. Today I call this same house my home.

I can only imagine the excitement of setting up a new house after spending the first years of marriage living in a hotel, maybe one room, in downtown Murdock. For a shopping trip to Willmar for the new house, Martin and Jennie brought along Mary McGinty Walsh, my great-grandmother, also their next-door neighbor, and Michael Walsh Jr., my great-grandfather. A few days later my grandparents hopped in their Ford, driving to Benson, the county seat of Swift County, to buy rugs to cover the wooden floors. I can only imagine how life must have been, moving into the white two-story wooden home with three bedrooms, kitchen, sitting room and dining room combined, for the young family with two small girls. A baby boy would join the Walsh family December 7, 1924; this was my father, Martin J. Walsh Jr., likely born in the front bedroom, the only bedroom on the first floor. The foundation of the house is made of fieldstone from a former flour mill that was located on the same location. Construction for the new house began or was completed in 1917, according to an inscription in the cellar.

There's not a lot I know about the hotel my grandparents lived in Murdock, only that it was likely on Main Avenue, also known as US Highway 12. Aunt Agnes, born October 18, 1916, and Aunt Margaret, born December 16, 1917, were both born at the hotel. I believe there were three hotels in Murdock, likely one for Catholics and one for Lutherans, but I've not confirmed the details. There is a photo hanging in the Post Office in Murdock with a glimpse of early Murdock, 1900s, likely one of the buildings was the location my aunts were born.

During the 1930s my family had lodgers, two schoolteachers, living with them, according to the 1930 US Census. When I read about the lodgers, I wondered which bedroom the teachers slept in. I think the three children slept in one room, maybe the larger south bedroom upstairs, and the teachers stayed in the smaller north bedroom upstairs, separated by the bathroom and landing. The north bedroom would eventually become my dad's room, painted in a light green color, the same as it is today. In my grandfather's final years—he lived to be one hundred, just short of 101 by a few weeks—he slept in the north bedroom, climbing the stairs to reach his room.

A piece I wrote about my grandfather when he turned one hundred was published in the Willmar, Minnesota, newspaper in 1987. My Aunt Margaret told me my grandfather would do exercises with his legs in bed, damaging the plaster on the walls. Margaret had the walls repaired in the 1980s, and I had the walls repaired again in 2010.

Moments in time have been preserved through the years, notably 1964, my first Christmas. One person missing from the series of photographs made from Kodachrome slides is my father, so he was likely busy taking photographs of my grandparents holding me, wearing a green dress and white tights, and my brother Paul, wearing coveralls in some photos, jeans or corduroy pants in others, and my mother, Margaret I. Walsh, not to be confused with my aunt, Margaret A. Walsh. In these photos, I see the sofa that is long gone, with only two people in the series of photographs still living, bringing tears to my eyes. In one of the photographs, my grandmother is holding me while I appear to put both of my tiny hands into my tiny mouth, while everyone is busy smiling for the camera, orchestrated by my father. There is one photo of my grandfather holding me wearing white pajamas in his left hand, while my brother is seated to the right, appearing to try to escape the photo opportunity, maybe wanting to grab my dad's 35mm camera. How lovely this family looks together in 1964.

I wish the people in this 1964 family Christmas photo session were all sitting with me now on the new sofa next to the staircase at home. I would say how much I love them all. Maybe I can just imagine they are surrounding me now, as sometimes I think they are with me, especially when I have thoughts in my mind recalling nostalgic family history, making me think I am not alone.

Home, Main Avenue, Murdock

If Dublin Farm was my grandfather's domain, then the family home located on Main Avenue on the edge of Murdock is the realm of Grandmother Jennie.

I sit in the living room at home in Murdock as I listen to a quiet house with the sounds of cars and farm trucks hauling loads of corn, soybeans, sugar beets and other crops to market. Outside my door I hear gears shifting from 30 mph to 60 mph, or just the reverse, 60 mph to 30 mph, as the house is located near the edge of village limits of Murdock. Officially Murdock is called a city, but I will still say it is a village as it was for years, with only 278 people.

The sunlight is flowing through the white sheer curtains in the combination living room and dining room, spreading light on the sofa, along with shadows from trees in the front yard. Branches are swaying up and down, to and fro. Outside it's 47 degrees, sunny, with winds west-southwest at 13 mph.

I draw open all the curtains and shades to let light fill the room divided by formal woodwork, with two wood columns, all darkly stained in mahogany or a deep brown color. The upright piano stands in one corner I played as a child, along with my brother, father, and aunts. Opposite of the piano, on the other side of the room, are two china cabinets, Grandfather's writing desk with covered compartments, and a folded dining table that hosted countless holidays and family gatherings. Covered underneath the green wool rug next to the writing desk, is a blue or black India ink stain caused by my brother Paul as a toddler exploring Grandfather's desk, leaving a permanent reminder of years past. If I want to see the stain today, I'd have to move the desk, and pull off the area rug. From my view near the china cabinets, I see the sunlight from the kitchen window and white lace curtains with flowers, rabbits, and gardens scenes.

September 16, 1922
"Moved some things into the Murphy House."

September 18, 1922
"Moved into Murphy house."

September 22, 1922
"Went to Willmar with mother (Mary McGinty Walsh) and Jennie. Jennie got a new coat."

September 23, 1922
"Went to Benson with Jennie. Got rugs for house."

According to the records, on June 19, 1923, at 4 pm, my grandmother Jennie Walsh purchased the family house from J. P. Murphy and Rose Murphy, his wife. Murphy is known for building many houses in the Murdock area, including the house next door, closest to the Catholic cemetery. The house was purchased for $3,500, with a mortgage of $2,500. It's likely my grandparents rented the house starting in September 1922, until my grandmother purchased the house, with payments coming from rent from Dublin Farm and my grandfather Martin's job with International Harvester. I can still remember the discovery after my grandmother's death of this interesting fact when my father talked about the ownership of the house by my grandmother; I had assumed my grandfather was the owner, or maybe both my grandparents. The discussion I recall from my parents and others indicated clever planning. Putting the ownership in my grandmother's name only was believed to help protect the family if my grandfather were sued or went bankrupt. This was also done to try to save Grandpa's bank shares if the bank failed and protect him from the bank coming after him personally for more money. I don't know if the practice would actually protect assets in my grandparents' day, but my grandparents kept their house, and I live in it today.

The reference to the Murphy House in my grandfather's diary is from the first owners of the house. *The Minneapolis Journal*, May 6, 1901, announced Murdock is to have a new fifty-barrel flour mill, to be erected by Albert Mahlow, along with other evidence of growth in Murdock, with an erection of a new three-story brick block building by James Clark Sr. and many new dwellings.

In 1905, Charles J. Macbeth, was the president of the Murdock Milling Company, and A. A. Macbeth was secretary, according to records filed at the Swift County Courthouse. February 11, 1905, the mill was sold for $10,000 to O. Bocklund and J. E. Pulver.

In 1911, Joseph S. Murphy acquired the land, and likely the remains from the Murdock Milling Company from John and Julia Taylor, then passed to Joseph P. Murphy in 1921 by way of a quitclaim deed without covenant for the sum of one dollar.

It was known from family stories my great-grandfather Stephen Foley worked at a flour mill in Murdock, making this very location also a place of employment, along with a place to live for my family. My grandfather Martin told me years ago the land where the house now stands was the site of an old flour mill, with part of the mill foundation used for the construction of the house, now confirmed with deed records.

The actual year the house transitioned from mill to house is not known, but there are clues in the cellar. If the morning light is just right, I can make out the markings of a window on the west side of the house in the cellar, nearest the electrical box. Inscribed in the cement covering a field stone wall foundation about three feet deep are the numbers: 1917 10/4. It is likely April 10, 1917, or October 4, 1917, but no doubt the year was 1917. Sometime in the late 1960s or early 1970s a cement floor was poured over the dirt floor, with the old woodburning range stove still standing in the center of the basement. About the same time the new floor came, a new entrance was added to access to the basement, through a breezeway to the garage. The cellar was entered originally from an outside wooden hatch door. Today, it's vital to duck your head before entering the cellar or suffer a bruised head.

<hr>

Tucked away in the modern kitchen cupboards is Grandmother Jennie's undated handwritten cookbook, I'm guessing from 1915 or so. This notebook is yellowed, with corners burnt, as I know there had been a fire in the kitchen. This cookbook was likely saved from destruction. I heard a story about a morning fire while my grandmother was cooking breakfast, likely a grease fire from bacon. The volunteer fire department arrived in the morning at the same time my grandfather was going to morning Mass. Instead of staying to help, my grandfather went to Mass, apparently saying, "Go on in, boys!" I can only think it must have been disturbing for my grandmother to have a kitchen fire and be left with fire fighters while your husband goes off to Mass.

During the Great Depression, hobos, or railroad tramps, came to the house for food served by my grandmother, according to my Aunt Margaret. It's likely the house was marked in some way to indicate my family's house served food to migrant workers or homeless people traveling from town to town, looking for work and a new start. The railroad tracks are directly across from the house on US Highway 12. A huge garden was located to the side of the house, no doubt a source of food for travelers when no one was looking.

⚜

My father was born at home in 1924. I asked my Aunt Margaret the exact location of my father's birth, and she thought the bedroom was the front bedroom, also the only bedroom on the first floor, just off of the living room and staircase to the second floor. I usually sleep in the front bedroom as in winter the room is warm, and cool in summer. The room where my father arrived in the world has morning light flowing in from the north and east windows when the curtains and shades are drawn open. There is a light fixture hanging from the ceiling with a string to pull, but there are small reading lights over the bed and on the night stand next to the bed. There's no closet, as the bedroom is small, but a small wooden wardrobe in the corner still contains one pair of my grandmother's shoes, and a few pieces of my clothing, like a night robe. The old chimney, no longer used, occupies a space in the corner next to the wardrobe; now there is central heating with an oil furnace for heating, along with a central air conditioner. A special wire trap was placed on the chimney, previously used for burning wood and coal, to stop bats from entering the house and flying around the living quarters. I can still remember my Aunt Margaret telling me about bats flying around the house while I was talking to her on the phone when I lived in Florida during the early 2000s. Sure enough, I found more dead bats in the house.

In this small front bedroom, I recall a memory of my grandmother

Jennie when I was a small girl, maybe six or seven years old. Grandmother had shingles and I was not allowed to enter the bedroom, but I attempted, and maybe succeeded. My Grandmother Jennie was in bed, while my mother told me to leave the room, in fear I might catch chickenpox. As a toddler, I can also remember my mother putting me down for naps in this same bedroom. This bedroom is where I rested for a few weeks after my father died in 2008. It was a room full of memories, one vital to the family.

Sitting on this same bed in the front bedroom, I remember working on a family history project as a student at St. Cloud State University in the mid-1980s, trying to piece together a family tree. I can remember when I asked my mother for help with dates and names. She would tell me to wait, and she would come back with the answers. I didn't know she was walking about the equivalent of one house away to Sacred Heart Cemetery to look at grave markers of my ancestors from Canada, Ireland, Scotland, Luxembourg, and more. The cemetery is now my form of outside family archives I visit often when I need to acquaint myself with a fact, a forgotten name or to pray at family graves.

As I sit on my bed, directly behind me is a headboard with a bookshelf filled with books. If I need to check family history late at night, I can slide the bookcase doors open, take out the Holy Bible, Douay Version. Written in the cover: Property of Mrs. M. J. Walsh, Murdock. There is no date the Bible was received or purchased by my grandmother, but there are three Imprimaturs, approval or license to print by the Roman Catholic Church, dated 1906, 1911, and 1912, appearing to be printed by the E. M. Lohmann Co., 413 15–17 Sibley St., St. Paul, Minnesota. It's possible this was a wedding gift from 1915, but that is only speculation.

A family record is located between the Old Testament and New Testament. The records are not all accurate, riddled with spelling and factual errors, adding challenges to recovering family records, along with the use of nicknames and abbreviations.

Husband: M. J. Walsh
Born: February 19, 1887, Dublin (Dublin Township)
Son of: Michael (Mike) Walsh, Mary Walsh

Wife: Mary Jannet (Jennie) Foley
Born: March 23, 1886
Daughter of Stephen Foley, Catherine Foley

Married: November 4, 1918, Murdock, Minnesota
Note: November 4, 1915 was actual date
By Rev. William Patrick (W. P.) Walsh
Sacred Heart Church

Children
Mary Agnes, October 18, 1916
Martin John, December 7, 1924
Margaret Anne, December 16, 1917

If my grandfather was gone on the road traveling for work, this certainly means my grandmother was working hard to raise three children on her own, during the Depression, deep in Minnesota farm country. She was clearly resourceful. The teachers who lodged with her likely influenced my aunts to become schoolteachers; both studied at St. Cloud Teachers College. There is wisdom from Grandmother Jennie's Bible I can find today with scraps of newspaper print marking pages, along with pencil marks around passages she read. One of the many pencil-marked verses found in my grandmother's Bible is this: "Hear in silence, and for thy reverence and good grace shall come to thee." (Ecclesiasticus 32:9, Douay)

I can hear the oil furnace running and feel the warmth coming from the vent next to the side of the bed. Last night I heard sounds of mice, like nails scratching in the basement or vents, but no mice have joined me in my bed yet.

❧

It's now about 2 pm, Saturday, October 13, 2018, and I'm standing outside the front door watching farm trucks carrying loads of corn and soybeans to the grain elevator a few blocks away in Murdock, located next to the railroad tracks. Trucks filled with the large brown sugar beets are turning south to a processing plant where mounds of sugar beets wait to be processed.

The steps off the front porch are covered in yellow and brown leaves, along with the sidewalk. I have no plans to rake the leaves as more will blow in from the neighbor's yards.

❧

I didn't know this home's address on Main Avenue until I moved to Murdock in 2010, but I had been coming to this house since I was a baby. I always sent mail to my grandparents and Aunt Margaret to the Post Office, so there was never a need to know a street address.

Besides not knowing the house number, I had no idea the road was called Main Avenue. Seven days after I arrived in Minnesota in 2010, I sold my house in Florida, and needed to sign papers for the house sale. I'm not sure how I determined the exact address for my aunt's house in Murdock, but likely from property tax papers, or went to the court house in Benson.

In my mind, I can see Joseph Foley and his wife, Marion, appearing at the front door like clockwork during my visits with my grandparents and Aunt Margaret, likely on Saturday or Sunday afternoon. My great-uncle Henry Walsh, my grandfather Martin's brother, lived next door with his wife Nora, famous for her cookies. As a little girl I would run next door for cookies. The house was originally owned by my great-grandparents. My great-grandfather purchased the lot for the house in 1899 for $50, a block away from Sacred Heart Catholic Church. The house for years was painted green, but is now a drab gray, with remains of spilled paint on the sidewalk.

❧

It's time to walk to the Post Office, about 4:30 pm, October 13, 2018, walking two or three blocks away from headquarters, what my Aunt Margaret called home in Murdock. I need to mail letters and bills. My family has had the same box number since 1953 or before, as my father's address was recorded at the Shelbourne Hotel in Dublin, Ireland guest registry as Murdock, Minnesota.

Several farm trucks pass by me as I walk against the wind on the way home. I can hear the humming from the grain elevator as loads of grain are dropped off by local farmers.

There are so many reasons to stay in the house I call home, the location my father was born, the location my family survived the Great Depression, Word War I and World War II is sacred. This is the home that gave shelter to neighbors during the 1940 Armistice Day blizzard when their furnace stopped working, along with feeding hobos and tramps. This is the home where we suffered and recovered from illnesses, prayed in secret at night looking for miracles, boarded teachers, raised three children, planned funerals, welcomed babies and new days. This is the home that sheltered my family, which survived and prospered through decades of storms. This home is sacred for my family, and all the lives we have encountered.

᪥

Sorting through the large dresser in the south bedroom in my grandparents' home in Murdock, I found a bottle of perfume with a label I could make out as Faberge, maybe Flambeau, but it is hard to see as the bottle is old. I wasn't sure if this belonged to Grandmother Jennie, Aunt Margaret, or if it was left by my Aunt Agnes during one of her trips home. The bottle had a small amount of perfume, so I opened it to smell.

The small bottle held a story of years gone by, likely was dabbed behind the ear or maybe on a hand before heading off to Mass at Sacred Heart Catholic Church, or a game of bridge, maybe even a visit of my own family as a little girl. The bottle could not disclose what important or insignificant events for which it prepared its users, but it did help uncover a story I still can recall from my childhood, all about a bottle of Joy perfume.

After finding the bottle of Faberge in the midst of sorting out the dresser drawers of clothing, photographs, letters and decades of memories tucked away in what might be a 1950s era dresser, complete with a double bed and second taller dresser, I found my mind transported to 1980, age sixteen, the summer before my junior year of Litchfield High School, in Litchfield, Minnesota.

My Aunt Agnes, Uncle Stanley, Aunt Margaret, brother Paul, and myself, were ready to return home from our trip to Ireland. In the remaining miles to Shannon Airport, I had uncontrollable hiccups, and drinking water did not solve them.

Just ahead of me on the tour bus were my aunts Agnes and Margaret, discussing their plans to buy a bottle of Joy perfume, somehow splitting the bottle between them. Now why can I remember such an odd story? I'm guessing the hiccups had me in some state of fear of flying home with hiccups. I already had tiny thorns in the palms of my hands from what was likely a seaside thistle or another small pink flower, which I got while sitting on large rocks along the west coast of Ireland overlooking the North Atlantic Ocean on the Ring of Kerry. The small thorns would travel in my hands from Ireland, only to be removed with help from my mother and a set of tweezers and a sewing needle to pry out the unwanted Irish souvenirs.

Shannon Airport was (and is) is famous for the duty-free shops, so my aunts knew they would find their bottle of Joy and avoid paying any duty charges. I can still remember asking my Aunt Agnes why she wanted to buy the perfume, still while I was busy with my hiccups. In the bus Agnes said it would be a treat, a reminder of the trip to Ireland. I can still see my aunts discussing the perfume on that summer day on the bus, like they were preparing for a mission or expedition. At least one or two bottles were purchased; now, the very smell of Joy triggers memories of my aunts, the 1980 trip to Ireland, and now the dresser drawer packed with memories in the south bedroom.

Joy perfume is not Irish, but had been a favorite of my aunts as long as I can remember, inhaled when I greeted them with hugs and kisses. Joy Eau de Toilette is really French, created during the Great Depression by Jean Patou in Paris, to help lift the spirits of his customers who were struggling but wanted to still have joy, made of jasmine flowers and roses.

This Depression-era perfume is the smell of my aunts, now my favorite and only perfume, made from over ten thousand jasmine flowers and roses, just for one ounce. Just before Christmas in 2010, I went in search of a bottle of Joy, finding it at the Nordstrom store at the Mall of America in Bloomington, Minnesota. At the perfume counter I smelled for the first time in twenty or more years the perfume of my aunts; it transported me to the 1980 trip to Ireland. I told the story to the woman helping me with the perfume, saying it was so important to me, and why finding the scent was so meaningful. I carry a small bottle with me in my toiletry bag, ready with a spray of Joy.

As I spray the scent on my hand, it is the roses I detect, but it's hard for me to discern the jasmine. It would almost seem this scent is magical in what it delivers, bringing the past to the present, making every trouble melt away.

All my thoughts of the past are triggered by a dresser drawer stuffed with forgotten artifacts and a Depression-era perfume with a light floral scent that's still being produced, transporting me through time and space, reuniting me with my father's sisters, my aunts of Joy.

Chapter 8

Aunt Agnes's Curriculum Vita[3]

Aunt Agnes's transcript of life, Saint John's University,
Master of Librarian Science, Saint Cloud Teachers College,
Bachelor of Science in Elementary Education

December 6, 2017
Miller Center, St. Cloud State University
St. Cloud, Minnesota

WALKING IN STORMY WEATHER IN MY DOWN-FILLED parka, stretching beneath my knees, on a cold Wednesday afternoon – December 6, 2017, to be exact – my body shivers and teeth chatter. I'm heading across the St. Cloud State University campus from my office in Stewart Hall where I'm an assistant professor, passing through Centennial Hall and Administrative Services to keep warm. The final destination is Miller Center's third floor, the location of University Archives. Every step in my winter boots seems to be an extra effort today, as I think of each building I pass through as my own personal warming house. The only exposed part of my body is my face, covered with my thickest wool scarf allowing only my eye glasses and a portion of my nose exposed to the winter elements; 17 degrees and chilling wind; my red hair is likely peeking out of my wool stocking hat, topped with my down-filled hood.

Entering Miller Center and finding my way to the elevator, thoughts about what I am doing and about to learn are running through my head. I'm about to learn details about my late Aunt Agnes, Mary Agnes Walsh (married name Mary Agnes Shopa), born 1916 and died 2003. Known by many as Agnes, the oldest sister of my late father, Martin J. Walsh Jr., both from Murdock, Minnesota,

---

3. Numerous documents from the University Archives at St. Cloud State University, along with the gracious help of University Archivist and Professor Tom Steman, were used in writing this chapter. https://www.stcloudstate.edu/library/archives/

located about eighty-five miles southwest of St. Cloud. Aunt Agnes was a student at the St. Cloud Teachers College from 1935 to 1939. My mission is to look at her academic transcripts, course work, grades and conferred degrees, with the idea of learning more details about one of my favorite aunts. The appointment gives me the excitement of a child about to see my aunt during one of her visits home to Murdock from Long Island, New York, where she worked as Chief Librarian at the Northport Veterans Hospital for almost forty years. She retired to Santa Barbara, California, the location she spent working during World War II as a US Marine. Agnes went on to receive a master of library science in 1957 at St. John's University in New York.

My appointment is 2 pm with University Archivist and Professor Tom Steman, someone I'm already acquainted with on campus. He had uncovered black and white photographs of me from my days working as a student photographer, about 1985 to 1986, at University Communication, showing off my long red curly hair, holding a Nikon film camera and rolling bulk reels of black and white film, obviously looking much younger and youthful.

Today was different. Today it was about Aunt Agnes, and what I might learn from college records. Minnesota state law allows me to see my aunt's academic records, as she has been deceased at least ten years and the data is at least thirty years old.

Before opening the door to the University Archives, I think about Agnes, and start to take off my winter outer garments, tossing them on to a chair in a pile, putting my backpack next to me. I ask myself if Agnes would want me to be digging around in her academic records, now almost eighty years old. She was a librarian, I am now in a university library, the very same college, now university, she attended, only with name changes since she attended. Agnes would be accustomed to requests for information, but today she is the subject. I answer my own question in my mind, by thinking Agnes would be happy I am interested in her, someone I talked to almost every weekend on the phone growing up. This is the same aunt who, as a girl, I practiced addressing envelopes and wrote letters to her home at Grover Lane, East Northport, New York, a short distance from her workplace at the Veterans Hospital in Northport. A Google search revealed the same Cape Cod style, two stories with dormer windows, looking almost as I remember from my summer visits. My brother Paul and I often flew there, staying a few weeks at the end of the summer before heading back to school in my hometown of Litchfield, Minnesota in the 1970s and 1980s.

❧

Today, I can still recall the floor plan at East Northport. The front door had a mail slot, with the letter carrier ringing the doorbell to signal delivery. As a girl, I marveled that the mail passed through the small opening, because this is how my aunt received my letters, such as my thanking her for birthday gifts. Mail at my home in Minnesota, on the other hand, was delivered to the post office in Litchfield. At Agnes's house, after entering the front door, to the left, was the living room with a formal dining room connected. The small kitchen had dark wooden cabinets, with a small kitchen table for two or more people, situated with a door to the backyard. A screened-in porch, located near the dining room, was fun place to sit in the afternoons to keep cool. The china cabinet from this particular dining room is now owned by me. It was originally purchased in 1967 at B. Altman and Co., Fifth Avenue at 34th Street, New York City, costing $366.34, and measuring sixty inches wide, according to the receipt tucked inside, along with a piece of my artwork as a child.

The master bedroom, bathroom and a small bedroom used as an office are located on the first floor. A staircase to the second floor was located near the front door, with a foyer, small area at the landing on the second floor. I slept on the second floor during my visits, with my suitcases tucked away in a storage space next to the roof. My aunt Agnes married when she was fifty years old, never having children, so my visits were extra special, likely because I was her only niece. In my adult years, older relatives would call me Agnes, as I look like her with red hair.

❧

Back to University Archives at St. Cloud State University, the archivist greets me, "I have your aunt's transcripts ready." It's not the tone of an undertaker, but the moment is serious. I think he is as excited for me to be there, ready to explore Agnes's records. As I look on the table, one large bound book measuring seventeen by thirteen inches, and about four inches thick, appears to look like an old ledger book, with a white sheet of paper marking my aunt's records. It is volume fifteen of some older college transcripts, marked on the spine, the back portion of the book's binding, in gold letters: State Teachers College, St. Cloud, Minnesota. There's a multicolored swirled design on the edges of the pages artistically decorated, creating a pattern of a marbled stone, alternating in colors. This is a serious looking book, containing intimate details of Agnes's college records, the results of her hard work as a young woman.

Volume 15 is opened by the archivist, and I'm looking on the right side of the page, that contains records of four students, total, with only my aunt's records revealed. The others are covered with white paper for privacy.

The transcript, page 533, has personal data, but not all is correct. She is listed as Agnes Mary Walsh, but she was actually Mary Agnes Walsh, known by family as Agnes. Mary was used for formal business, and her late husband, Stanley Shopa Sr. called her Mary, insisting only to call her Mary, causing me heartache and confusion as a child, as I had an Aunt Agnes, not Aunt Mary. Her date of birth is incorrect, listed as October 18, 1917, but was actually October 18, 1916. She was admitted to the State Teachers College on September 13, 1935, attended College of St. Catherine in St. Paul, 1934 to 1935, now known as St. Catherine University, or simply St. Kate's, earning thirty quarter hours during her time in St. Paul.

What's not listed is the story behind St. Kate's, as told to me as a child more than once. Agnes's grade reports from St. Kate's are tucked away upstairs in a chest in the home attic in Murdock. I live now in the same house as my aunts and father lived, the same place my father was born. Family folklore has it that it was difficult for Agnes to achieve high scores as did wealthy and privileged college girls. This prompted her transfer to the St. Cloud State Teachers College in 1935, the same year her sister Margaret Anne Walsh, started as a freshman. The story of the academic difficulties was told to me more than once as a child. I never asked Agnes about the story when she was alive, but wish today she could tell me more about her year at St. Kate's, 1934 to 1935.

The St. Cloud transcript lists Agnes's religion as Catholic, with nationality of her father as Irish and mother as Irish and German. On nationality, it does not note her parents were born in United States, as today nationality is what's listed on a passport, country of birth, not countries of origin of the family. Her mother's nationality, actually heritage, is only half correct: it should be Irish and Luxembourger, not German. Agnes' grandmother was noted for her French style cooking, likely meaning she had French heritage, from Luxembourg, a small European country between

Germany, France, and Belgium. It had established independence from the French Empire in 1815, later to be occupied by the German Reich during World War II.

M. J. Walsh, Martin J. Walsh, Agnes's father and my grandfather, is listed as parent, not mentioning her mother's name, Jennie Foley Walsh, simply with the address as Post Office, Murdock, no mention of a box office box number.

Just above a double red line, almost pink, lists Aunt Agnes's degrees. She graduated from a two-year course in Elementary and Rural Education, November 25, 1936, with 105 quarter hours. Her second degree, is listed as bachelor of science in elementary education, graduating in November 29, 1939, with 193 quarter hours.

Below the double red line, is a list of her college course work, including her high school courses from Murdock High School, where she graduated in 1934. Courses Agnes had in Murdock included algebra, biology, home economics, English, general science, geography, geometry, history, Latin, and sociology for a total of sixteen credits.

Agnes was very busy over the course of her studies, with the goal of becoming a school teacher. The campus laboratory school was located in Riverview, a building where students observed experienced teachers in the classroom and also practice teaching as students. Agnes's transcript of 193 quarter hours include education, English, industrial arts, languages, mathematics, music, physical education, science, and social science.

In the 1936 *Talahi*, the yearbook at St. Cloud Teachers College, Agnes was a sophomore, listed as a member of Yo-Hi Club, a group for girls not living on campus; Newman Club, a Catholic college organization; and Rural Life Club, for students pursuing teaching positions in rural areas. Her portrait, about age nineteen, is very sweet, with a short bob hair cut with a wave, with her bangs sweeping to the side, modeled after starlets like Bette Davis or other Hollywood darlings. The yearbook takes its name from Talahi Woods on campus, situated next to the Mississippi River and Riverside Park, with views of Beaver Island, still popular locations for students and class field trips.

⚜

In 1937, after receiving a two-year degree in 1936, Agnes was teaching in De Graff, a village a few miles from her hometown of Murdock, according to the May 28, 1937, *The College Chronicle*. This is the same college newspaper I worked for as a student at St. Cloud State. I encountered a student of Agnes's a few years ago while visiting the Church of St. Bridget in De Graff. An elderly woman, likely in her seventies or eighties, was preparing flowers for the church, while a young man was vacuuming. The woman started talking to me while I was looking over the stained glass windows, especially the window featuring St. Patrick, donated by my great-grandfather Patrick "Paddy" McGinty. I can't remember the woman's name at this time, but do recall the story she told me about a man offering her and her brother a ride home. They refused to take the ride, only to find out it was my grandfather Martin Walsh Sr., likely on his way to pick up Agnes from her teaching job in De Graff, placing the time to about 1937. What was interesting was she remembered my grandfather had a truck, one can only guess it was a Ford.

⚜

The 1940 United States Census lists Agnes, age twenty-three, living at home with her parents, Martin J. Walsh, age fifty-three, and Jennie Walsh, age fifty-four, along with her brother Martin, age fifteen, my father. Agnes is working as a public school teacher, likely in De Graff or Murdock. During the 1930 census, two lodgers lived with the family, both teachers, Verna Lindberg and Mary Walsh, unknown if related, but most likely as most the Walshes in Murdock were related. Agnes, age thirteen, was most likely influenced at home by the in-house teachers. The sleeping arrangements must have been tight, as there are three bedrooms in a small house, and seven people were living in the house in 1930. It wasn't until the 1960s the house was remodeled to add a bathroom on the first floor.

⚜

The St. Cloud Teachers College campus still has glimpses of the campus of Aunt Agnes's time of graduation in 1939, and University Archives helped splice together history. Lawrence Hall is still a dormitory, housing about one hundred students, as well as academic offices, along with Shoemaker Hall, built in 1915, where I spent my junior year living on campus. The library was housed at the Old Model School when Agnes was a student. Eastman Hall had classrooms, a swimming pool and gym. It is the likely location Agnes took required swimming lessons for her teaching studies, also where I swam as student. Riverview was the model school where Agnes watched experienced teachers in classrooms and became a student teacher, along with her sister Margaret. During my freshman year, 1982, I had an 8 am class in English composition on the first floor of Riverview.

History lives and breathes on the campus where Agnes studied. Burying or hiding the past will eventually surface, as did the grave sites of St. Cloud's first Protestant cemetery, 1856 into 1864. The site was discovered during the building of the Miller Center in 1999. This is the current location of the campus library and archives. The graves were previously partially covered by a parking lot I used as a student. The bodies from the graves were re-interned, moved about two miles west of campus to North Star Cemetery, St. Cloud.

The 1935 student directory from University Archives provided a glimpse to where Agnes lived, giving an interesting look to the changing campus and surrounding neighborhood. Agnes lived in 1935 at 630 Second Avenue South, St. Cloud, a house that's long gone. My best estimation for my aunt's accommodations is the current location of Centennial Hall, opened in 1971 to celebrate the University's one-hundredth anniversary, serving as the campus library when I studied and worked as an undergraduate student, 1982 to 1986, and spending countless hours studying.

I think Agnes would have been pleased to know the place where she once slept would become a library, as she spent almost her adult life as a librarian, except for her years teaching grade school. Today Centennial has the Herberger Business School and other academic offices in the five-floor brick and concrete building. The other possibility of the house is just north of Centennial, a location called Atwood Mall, situated between Atwood Memorial Center and the Performing Arts Center.

Agnes grew up on Main Avenue in Murdock; Minnesota-born author Sinclair Lewis penned a book with a similar name, *Main Street*. Not far from my aunt's student housing, a few blocks away or about a five-minute walk, is the Lewis House, 724 Fourth Avenue South, St. Cloud. The Tudor Revival-style house was home to Claude Lewis, local physician and brother of the famed author Sinclair Lewis, 1930 winner of the Nobel Prize in Literature, and known to often stop in to visit, according to University Archives, St. Cloud University. Sinclair Lewis wrote the book *Main Street*, had the main character as a country doctor, potentially modeled after Claude, with a setting called Gopher Prairie, Minnesota, modeled after Sauk Centre, Minnesota. I wonder if Agnes caught a glimpse of Sinclair out and about St. Cloud as he worked on his novels. She could have been a character in a novel as a Minnesota college student teacher from small town Murdock. Family discussions, especially with my late mother, Margaret I. Walsh, revealed that reading *Main Street* was prohibited, as many of the characters were thought to be based on real people. My mother often repeated the story as a girl in the 1930s and 1940s about her late uncle James "Jim" Rooney from rural Brooten, Minnesota, and their visits to Sauk Centre. He was able to identify the real people, or maybe just made good guesses, from Sauk Centre portrayed in *Main Street*. I now wish I had written down the names my mother repeated as they are lost in time. There is no longer fear, and I have a few books from this famous author, including *Main Street*. My mother also repeated a story related to *Main Street* about Dr. Claude Lewis, likely in late 1940s or early 1950s. During this time, she was a religious sister with the Franciscan Sisters of Little Falls, Minnesota, but never took final vows. She worked in a nursing home in Little Falls and also at St. Cloud Hospital, often staying with patients about to die. My mother's words about Sinclair's brother the doctor were almost always the same from her days as a nun: "He had wild, crazy red hair!" Sinclair and Claude both had red hair, according to their 1942 World War II draft cards.

❧

The bed I sleep in at home in Murdock has a bookcase as part of the headboard, dating back to the 1950s. It just happens to be the same bed I like to read and write from, as it is comfortable. Directly behind me is the bookcase, where I can slide a door to reveal books read by my family, including a Bible with my name written at my birth in 1964. Sinclair Lewis is represented in this bookcase with *Cass Timberlane*, published in 1945. The following is found in the opening pages: "This is a wartime book. The text is complete and unabridged, but every effort has been made to comply with the Government's request to conserve essential materials." The discarded book is marked Property of Plant 2 Library, Grumman Aircraft Eng. Corp., Bethpage, Long Island, New York, complete with a bookmark between pages 291 and 293, likely marking the last reader, from 1963 National Library Week, encouraging reading.

During World War II, Agnes served her country as a United States Marine Corps Corporal, stationed near Santa Barbara, California, in Goleta. I understand she worked as a librarian and other duties as a marine, but experienced a part of history, with newspaper clippings stashed away in family archives. In 1942 Agnes was in Santa Barbara when a Japanese submarine attacked an oil field along the coastline of the Pacific Ocean. This was the first time since 1812 the United States mainland was attacked by another country. I can still remember talking to Agnes about the shell attacks, noting she was not injured. They occurred as the same time as one of President Roosevelt's Fireside Talks, about 7 pm, February 23, 1942, according to Goleta Valley Historical Society. Agnes's marine uniform was stored for years in an attic closet in Murdock. Only a few items survive with it, such a purse, hat, marine insignias. I wore one of her fitted wool suits in high school from the 1940s or 1950s. I wanted to wear her uniform, but it was too small for me. Agnes's sister Margaret A. Walsh joined her in Santa Barbara, arranging for Margaret to work as a school teacher, as there was a need to help the war effort with military families living and working in the area.

Agnes's early adult years would influence her to return to Santa Barbara in the 1980s, living at Willowglen Road, located just off of Foothill Road, with a view of the San Marcos Foothills. If you look just right, you could catch a glimpse of the Pacific Ocean through the kitchen window. She lived on Willowglen Road until she moved to her last residence, Valle Verde, a nursing home and retirement community. I would visit her in 2001, my last time to see her alive.

The Old Mission in Santa Barbara was a place Agnes loved to take me for Mass, usually on Saturday night, followed by going to her favorite restaurant on State Street called Harry's Plaza Cafe, with a standing order for a reserved table for years. The walls are covered with photographs of celebrities, including movie star President Ronald Reagan. When Reagan visited his ranch near Santa Barbara, Agnes would say all the president's men were not far away.

In the summer of 1984, Olympians from around the world stayed at the Olympic Village at the University of California, Santa Barbara. I spent that summer staying at Willowglen Road, while taking a summer class. It was an exciting experience as I had the opportunity to hold the Olympic torch while it passed through the campus, located next to the Pacific Ocean. The summer experience helped me develop my photography skills, and launch my career in photojournalism on campus, start working at the student newspaper, *The University Chronicle*, when I returned to fall semester at St. Cloud State.

After World War II, Agnes found work as Chief Librarian at the Northport Veterans Administration Hospital. Her skills as a librarian were apparently outstanding, as she was selected by the Division of Library Extension of the New York State Library in

Albany, New York to instruct at a 1957 workshop for Institutional librarians, with special training for librarians, nurses, occupational therapists, social workers, and volunteers. A newspaper clipping notes Agnes was selected to instruct at the workshop because of her outstanding leadership in library work as a consultant in the metropolitan area and with the Veterans Administration, according to Arnold A. Schillinger, manager of the Northport Hospital. The workshop was at St. Lawrence University, in Canton, New York, July 21 to 26, 1955.

Universitas Sancta Joanns Neo-Eboraci Magistratumin Bibliothecali Mary A. Walsh die XVI Junii Anno Domini MCMLVII

Two summers later, Agnes received her master's degree in library science from St. John's University in New York City, June 16, 1957. Her rolled, large diploma, with her name written on the outside in pencil, Mary Walsh, is currently tucked away in a file cabinet at home in Murdock. It's written in Latin, adding more intrigue. Was the graduation ceremony conducted in Latin? Or perhaps at least for conferring of degrees, along with exploring her course work, especially to find Latin played a role in her graduate degree, as she worked closely with medical staff.

Aunt Agnes served as president of the Association of Hospital and Institution Libraries from 1967–1968, a division of American Library Association (ALA) at the time. She also served as vice president and president-elect, 1966–1967, and past president, 1968–1969, according to the ALA archives. This was while she was chief librarian at the US Veterans Administration Hospital in Northport. I recall my mother telling me this fact and that it was confirmed by my Aunt Margaret, indicating it was a very political time period.

Agnes was a smart dresser, always wearing a fitted suit during her visits home to Minnesota, with often a matching handbag and shoes, always well heeled. Her hair was well coiffed, having her hair routinely set. Her height was shorter than me, possibly about 5'2". What she lacked in statue, was made up by her mind and education. She was a woman who encouraged me as a child and adult, but served as an inspiration to others she encountered, with soft spot for disadvantaged individuals. I watched her in the late 1980s or early 1990s once help a young mother struggling to get across the street, holding her baby, appearing to about to fall over, likely from hunger at

Stearns Wharf, the intersection of State Street and Cabrillo Boulevard, Santa Barbara. Before I could help, Agnes already crossed the street with the mother and baby, likely giving her money to eat. There are similar situations I recall witnessing, not completely understanding why she was helping and the urgency to help. I would say I do try to act as quickly as possible when strangers are struggling near me, likely because of Aunt Agnes.

The late Mary Rutledge was known as the dressmaker or seamstress in Murdock, a bit fragile as she suffered from polio, but still active, and sewing dresses for ladies. As a small girl, I accompanied Aunt Agnes a few times for a fitting at Mary's home, likely in 1960s or 1970s, located on Main Avenue in Murdock, not far from the Catholic church. The picturesque little white house, complete with a porch and finishing of gingerbread, or lattice, making the visit even more grand. Agnes would shop for her goods, what she called the yards of fabric, in New York City department stores, sending it home to Mary before arriving for her visit. Sewing patterns, and notions such as buttons and zippers, all were delivered to Mary. I look back now and think my Aunt Agnes likely could have purchased what she wanted at a fancy department store, but it was Mary who would sew her fitted suits for work as the chief librarian at the Northport Veterans Hospital. The outfits likely made Aunt Agnes look good and reminded her of home, but I think it was also a way to help Mary financially, giving her esteem and a great boast from the east coast to tiny Murdock, hidden Minnesota farm country.

⚜

There is an old photograph on top of the upright piano in the living room of two small children, Agnes and her sister Margaret, dated June 1918. Agnes and Margaret often traveled together around the world to Europe, Asia and the United States, as they had done for years, collecting souvenirs to send home to family members. It was 1980 at age sixteen, I had the chance to join my Aunts Agnes and Margaret on my first trip to Ireland.

In smartly dressed suits, I can see my aunts, the two sisters, walking in Dublin, Ireland in 1980, likely Brown Thomas department store on Grafton Street or Clerys on O'Connell Street, shopping enjoying life as grand as it could be, visiting the Abbey Theatre, Phoenix Park, and touring Trinity College Library to see the *Book of the Kells*. Today my aunts are both gone, but live on in my memories, along with my Uncle Stanley, husband of Aunt Agnes.

꧁

Aunt Agnes died at Valle Verde in Santa Barbara with her sister Margaret at her side. There was a prayer and rosary service the night before her funeral, with an old Irish priest officiating, seemingly only appropriate for my Agnes, with family Irish heritage. The morning of Thursday, November 13, 2003, was very emotional at her funeral. It was likely before the start of the funeral a woman attending the funeral Mass came up to me and said, "Your mother was very religious. She attended Mass a lot. I'm so sorry for your loss." I didn't have the strength to say I was not her daughter and simply thanked her.

The woman in the church was right in many ways, as Agnes was like a mother to me. I was the daughter she never had. We looked alike, had similar facial features and red hair, and people at home in Murdock called me Agnes at times.

During Aunt Agnes's funeral, I recall walking behind the casket as it was rolled to the front of the altar, there is little else I can recall as I was crying for most of the funeral. My Aunt Margaret was seated next to me always, and I need to help her, as she was in her mid-eighties. There was a moment when things were so beautiful, with light streaming in from the side windows, falling directly on Agnes's coffin. If a funeral can beautiful, it was that very moment, a sign of hope on that day for myself and Aunt Margaret.

Burial was at Riverside National Cemetery in Riverside, California, alongside her late husband Stanley, about 158 miles from Santa Barbara. Aunt Margaret and I rode upfront with the undertaker and Aunt Agnes in the back of the hearse. Using my mobile phone, I called my father back home in Minnesota during the ride to let him know we were heading to the cemetery and wanted to make sure he understood what was to happen. It was actually an enjoyable ride, as the young undertaker was very agreeable and friendly the entire drive. I looked back several times, though, with disbelief that Agnes was dead, in her coffin, and we were on our way to bury her.

At Riverside National Cemetery we were met by another Catholic priest to officiate the interment, the Rite of Committal. There was a small service at a location near the gravesite. Aunt Margaret talked briefly about all of her sister's friends and family, and her huge Christmas card list and correspondences. It was Aunt Agnes encouraging me as a small girl to write her at Grover Lane, East North Port, New York, living most of her adult life away from her native Murdock. Now it was final, and Agnes was about to be put to rest far away from home.

There were concerns about Agnes's burial, by Aunt Margaret and myself. According to the rules of the national cemetery, family was not allowed to be next to the open grave. There were several funerals going on, there was concern Agnes would not be buried in her own grave. This was not Murdock, and the national cemetery was overwhelming. I had to insist to be able to see Agnes's open grave with her coffin in it. I heard the cemetery officials making a fuss, using code or slang, such as family wanting to go to the open grave site. In the end, Aunt Margaret and I were allowed to go to the open grave, toss a few roses on her casket already in the ground, and say a few final and personal prayers.

⚜

The reality of final exam week is upon me, starting on December 11, 2017, at St. Cloud State University, not unlike exam weeks during Aunt Agnes's time at St. Cloud Teachers College, including the cold and snowy winter conditions. I will be grading student work, issuing final grades that will appear in their academic transcripts, that will have bearing on future careers and educational plans.

What I must say about the findings of Aunt Agnes's transcripts record from St. Cloud Teachers College is I did find factual errors about her personal information, not about her actual grades, as there's no way to verify, or check the grades for accuracy, only what is recorded. It is Agnes's transcript of life and how she lived it, loved it and reached out for people in need, including myself, and strangers. Her library skills went beyond her home, reaching to the East Coast in New York as part of Veteran's Administration, and to the West Coast, during the Word War II, in Santa Barbara, as part of the United States Marine Corps.

Aunt Agnes bought me a special outfit the summer I started as a freshman at St. Cloud State University, fall 1982. In Santa Barbara, located on State Street at Lou Rose Dress Shop, a road lined with buildings in Spanish Colonial Revival architecture, I selected a tan corduroy skirt with yoke waist with button closure, a pair of shoes, and a wool purple sweater with my initial embroidered. The sweater was worn for years, mended several times in the elbows, as I wore almost daily to classes and everywhere during my freshman year. The sweater and outfit made me feel very special and loved. Lou

Rose Dress Shop just happened to be Agnes's favorite dress shop. I remember the ladies helping me were serving Agnes glasses of wine while I was busy in the dressing rooms, something I had never experienced in my life. This was very different from the dressmaking experience back in Murdock. This ladies dress shop was like a stand in for Mary Rutledge's home where cups of tea might be served, not wine, the latest news from Murdock, and lengths of hemlines for the season are rising or falling.

Thank you, Aunt Agnes, for a life well lived. You are truly missed.

Chapter 9

Aunt Margaret

Aunt Margaret's Final Trip to Europe
New Coat from Harrods, 1996

MY AUNT MARGARET'S SPECIAL BLUE COAT WAS PUR-chased at Harrods, a famous department store located on Brompton Road in Knightsbridge, London. The date of purchase was December 5, 1996. Margaret was days short of seventy-nine years of age; I was living in the Netherlands, 1994–1997, and Aunt Margaret came to visit me for about a month.

In London, we stayed at the Union Jack Club in Waterloo, with quick access to the London Underground Tube, the public rapid transit system, finding our way to Harrods. After a few hours of going through the coats at Harrods, she settled on the navy-blue Burberry coat with two large pockets with flaps, collar and sleeves with a brown corduroy trim. The length of the coat needed to be altered and would require a few hours of work. Harrods had a tailor shop to take care of the alternations, meaning we had more time to kill at the department store lunchroom.

It was the first time in my life I saw the letter H, standing for Harrods, dusted in the hot foamed milk of my cappuccino, likely with chocolate, also so delightful, I didn't want to drink the artwork. I'm sure we had lunch—soup and sandwiches—but after several years, the H stands out so clear.

After lunch Margaret and I went to the food halls in Harrods where delicacies from around the world were sold, including teas and coffees. I still have an original green tea caddy labeled Harrods Knightsbridge, Mango & Passion Fruit, almost a full container. It was also the first time in my life I'd seen tea with fruit, so it was an incredible wonder. According to the label, it was purchased at almost 2 pm, on December 5, 1996.

Today, December 10, 2017, more than two decades ago, I make the same tea I purchased with Aunt Margaret here at home in Murdock. First, I pry open the very tight lid on the green tin tea caddy with a screwdriver. When I open it there is smell of fruit, and the contents are dry. After waiting for the kettle to whistle, and water boil on the stove, I let the tea steep for about ten minutes before testing it. The tea is noticeably fruity, with a light brown color. Not knowing the tea's provenance, I'd say it was just a weak tea. I think Aunt Margaret might have enjoyed a sip of the Harrods tea in her Currier and Ives blue teacups and saucers, as I am doing today. I'll now have another cup of tea as the taste improves when it steeps for several minutes or even an hour or more.

Aunt Margaret's winter boots were also part of the items to sort through from her nursing home room after her death, part of the winter weather kit Margaret was wearing in Europe in 1996. I'm not sure what happened to her boots; they were likely donated to charity.

During Margaret's final trip to Europe, a zipper on her boot broke or got stuck, and there was no way to pull her boot off. It was a bit perplexing and the only solution was to go to a shoe repair shop in Sittard, The Netherlands. The shop was equipped with stools, something like we would see at a bar in the United States, for repairs on footwear as you waited. I dropped Aunt Margaret off at the shop and returned about an hour later. Like a surgeon, the Dutch shoe specialist cut Margaret out of her boot and replaced the zipper. She was wearing the same boots from 1996, or before, to 2010 when she went into the nursing home, as the boots were the one pair of shoes she could get on her feet. Margaret walked in these boots for fourteen or fifteen years, traveling beyond the United States to England, France, Belgium, the Netherlands, and Germany, and back home in Murdock.

Just before Christmas in 1996, we were visiting a Christmas market in Valkenburg, the Netherlands, located in what is called the Velvet Caves, used during World War II to shelter people, including American troops. I recall enjoying a bowl of split pea soup with a large slice of ham, crying and explaining to Aunt Margaret how homesick I was for the United States. She just listened to me talk, as she did with many military veterans when she worked as a social worker for the Veterans Administration, except I was her niece. She was always willing to listen to my stories and struggles, as she did for many years.

Aunt Margaret's Last Christmas
Extra Wool Socks for Minnesota Burial

Margaret A. Walsh, 95
December 16, 1917 to December 3, 2013
All this living of Margaret was happening in an area of just a few blocks, complete with merchants, a church, and a Catholic cemetery

marking western boundary of Murdock. It was not until 2013 that Aunt Margaret took up her final resting place in the cemetery.

Keeping Vigil at Bethesda Heritage Center, Willmar, Minnesota
Night of December 2, 2013, and Early Morning December 3, 2013

It was early in the morning, about 1 or 2 am, and I was sleeping in Aunt Margaret's room at Bethesda Heritage Center, a nursing home in Willmar, Minnesota, about fifteen miles west of Murdock on US Highway 12. I had been sleeping in a reclining chair, keeping warm with a sleeping bag and pillow I tucked away behind the chair during the day. I had my little eleven-pound dog Bobby with me, a Yorkshire Terrier Mix breed, keeping me company with his own little round bed located near the recliner. Bobby needed to be kept on his leash at the nursing home as he enjoyed visiting residents in other rooms. In fact, he once walked across the hall off his leash, visiting at least one elderly resident, sleeping under a bed, until he was discovered by a nurse, very surprised to find Bobby comfortable at the nursing home.

My aunt had her hospital-style bed with the moving parts to raise and lower her head and feet. There was a wardrobe with her clothing, all labeled with her name. A television set was placed on top of her dresser drawers so she could watch as she pleased. This was a final of a series of about three rooms she lived in at Bethesda for almost three years, starting in early 2010. She wanted this specific room, as there was a private bathroom; there was always a waiting list for this room, an opening almost always filling when a resident died.

That night was different than any other, as this might be the night Margaret would die. She is ninety-five years, diagnosed with liver cancer about two months earlier, in October 2013. After Margaret's face and skin started to turn yellow, she was rushed to Rice Memorial Hospital in Willmar; tests revealed the cancer and the reason for her yellow complexion, called jaundice, with no chance of recovery. Her Certificate of Death lists cause of death as pancreatic cancer; the medical examiner listed her cause of death as natural, but there seems to be nothing natural concerning cancer and death.

In the time after Margaret's terminal diagnosis, her mind started to change more; she asked the same questions again and again, or repeated stories she just told. During this time period Margaret would sing in her bed, as if with an alternative church service—there was no television or radio, it only existed in her mind. Margaret would announce the hymn and lead the singing. "Please turn to page 350," a random number in her mystical hymnal, follow by what came to her, "Holy, holy, holy. . . ." Each time her personal Mass began, I watch and listened, never questioning or correcting her, just sat and listened. It usually lasting no more than five minutes. I can only imagine that she thought she was seated in the family pew at Sacred Heart Catholic Church in Murdock with her family. The church during her childhood had assigned pews, with parishioners paying rent, as a way to pay off the mortgage for the church. My family was assigned about the fifth pew, left side looking at the altar, as I was told by a few church members, but the actual numbers were removed during recent remodeling in early 2000s.

Sometime in the early hours of December 3, 2013, likely about 2 am, I woke up from sleeping in the reclining chair to check on Aunt Margaret, but only to find her hand and face were cold. At this moment, I believed she might have died. I walked into the hall to find a nurse to help me. Not one, but two nurses arrived to check on Margaret, confirming she had died. I seem to recall that they immediately expressed condolences and sorrow, hugging me. My life at this very moment changed, as my duties as Margaret's guardian were complete. There was a strange sense of freedom and peace overshadowing the grief that had not yet arrived. The middle of the night death was very peaceful for Margaret, as I was sleeping just a few feet away, missing her last grasps of air and not holding her hand as she departed from earth. I was just unable to sit by her bed and wait for her moment of death as my own sleep was required. For this, I hope Margaret understands I needed to sleep.

After Margaret died, the nurses asked me to leave her room so they could clean and prepare her. The undertaker from Benson, Minnesota, was on the way, about a thirty-minute car drive away, and would be arriving to take Margaret to Benson for final preparation.

About fifteen minutes later, I returned to her room to wait with Margaret until the undertaker arrived, resting in the recliner chair, drifting in and out of sleep, with my dog Bobby curled up in his bed. Margaret looked at peace in her bed, covered with a white cotton blanket. The lights were low and the lights from a small Christmas tree were blinking on and off.

The Christmas tree was something I arranged to have delivered to Margaret's room as soon as she had returned from the hospital after her diagnosis for cancer in October of 2013, as I knew the following days were going to be very difficult.

In previous years, I'd helped Margaret prepare her Christmas cards with addresses and stamps, with the task of just signing her name, something she looked forward to doing, at a small lap table. It was a great activity to connect with family and friends, almost always resulting in receiving a card. The year 2013 was very different as Margaret lacked even the energy to sign her name, but I managed to have her sign two Christmas cards, one for my brother Paul and myself. Her signature very difficult to make out, with "Mar" separated from "garet." The last name of Walsh was more just Wals, hard to make out the h. I remember telling Margaret she would only need to fill out two Christmas cards and I would take care of the rest. I knew these were the last Christmas cards she would ever sign, maybe the last example of her signature. She executed her signature with all her might, trying to move the black ink pen to make the name she had signed all her life, no different than for a legal document, but on a Christmas card. Today I keep the card in a china cabinet at home in Murdock, with a scene of the Virgin Mary holding baby Jesus, both riding on a donkey, with Joseph and his walking stick, and the Star of Bethlehem overhead in the sky.

Aunt Margaret had been living at Heritage Center since 2010. The word Bethesda comes from the Bible, chapter five of the book of John. Bethesda is a Hebrew word for pool, and is associated with a sheep gate in Jerusalem, believed to be a place for healing the ill, blind, lame, and crippled, with the specific story of Jesus healing a lame man after thirty-eight years of illness, asking him to rise up and walk, and he does so. I knew all too well the reality Margaret could not be cured, or receive surgery, but could only be kept comfortable. She understood her illness, comprehending that she was dying, with no question of what more could be done when the doctor delivered her personal sentence to death. It was me who asked what more could be done. Margaret's nursing home did not offer Irish healing wells, and was beyond any cure the waters might offer.

Stepping back to the moment when she was diagnosed with cancer, my burdens seemed so heavy, and I thought I would need to deliver the bad news to Margaret. I can still remember saying to her doctor, "Do I need to tell her she has cancer?" I further prepared the physician for the delivery, as if I was working on a crisis communication case in my realm of public relations. I said to the doctor, "Make sure you say she will be comfortable in her rooms." I learned not to challenge her, simply agreeing. She likely helped hundreds or thousands of military service veterans at various veterans hospitals around the country, retiring after thirty years of service in 1982 in Des Moines, Iowa. If Margaret's room had to be compared to anything, I'd say that a college dorm room would be a very close comparison, except graduation from the nursing home for Margaret was eternity.

I know I called for a Catholic priest to come to the hospital or the nursing home to give Margaret the Sacrament of Last Rites, considered vital to make a journey into eternity, a bit like making final travel arrangements for Catholics, with the destination as heaven.

Now back to the arrival of the young undertaker; he was maybe about thirty years old or so. He was startled when he arrived in Margaret's room to see my dog jump out of his bed to greet him in the early hours of December 3. This became my cue to depart and leave Margaret and finish the rest of the night in my own bed in Murdock. I put on my down parka and winter boots, and a winter coat on my dog, and we drove home in Margaret's white 1998 Volvo. In my mind, my job as guardian was complete. I was both relieved and confused about Margaret's death, although it was very clear she was at peace, and no longer suffering. There simply was too much to process in the early hours of the day and sleep was the best solution for any complex thinking.

The next morning I went to the nearby funeral home in Benson and delivered Margaret's clothing for the funeral, along with a rosary and other items I had stored away for almost three years in a travel garment bag. In 2010, when I went to Ireland, I had to make sure people were taking care of my house, and they knew the exact location of Margaret's burial outfit. I selected a white silk blouse and a green tweed suit, with jacket and skirt, all from Pendleton, an American woolen mill that's been in business for about as long as my family has lived in Murdock. I wanted to make sure Margaret looked good, a nice suit of clothes for travel and be prepared to look her best for her funeral and final journey.

***

Shortly after I arrived home in Minnesota to live in 2010, I encountered two elderly ladies at a cafe in Kerkhoven, a small town just east of Murdock about three miles often called by locals just Kerk. After finishing a meal, I was getting my coat on, and ladies started to talk to me, likely to find out my name as I was stranger to them. I shared my name, and that my aunt was Margaret Walsh in Murdock, not saying she was in a nursing home. I don't think the ladies shared their names, but instead started to talk poorly of my aunt and how she dresses. It was true Margaret was only wearing the same pieces of clothing in the final days before entering the nursing home, something that I understand was very common. I let the two ladies continue to talk about my aunt, and didn't know how to reply to their continued degrading comments.

Then it came to me that I would pay them a compliment, but was not intended to be complimentary. I said something like this, "You are both right. Margaret is not as fashionable as you two fine ladies." It was when I told them Margaret was in the nursing home in Willmar, and that they seemed to be surprised, and their laughter and chuckling stopped. I never encountered the two ladies again. This situation made me think quickly as I was my aunt's guardian, and also handling her public relations at the café in Kerk and beyond.

⚜

I thought Margaret needs something more for her final journey. I wasn't sure what would work, so I gave a few pair of wool socks to the undertaker with the instructions to return what wasn't needed. The extra socks never were returned, but I know the exact location. I'm just unable to retrieve them, due to the fact they are buried with Margaret.

The wake or visitation was the night before Margaret's funeral at Sacred Heart Catholic Church. Very few people made a showing due to the cold subzero temperatures, maybe a dozen or so people coming. The undertaker put the bag of extra socks in the coffin for safe keeping, buried with Margaret, just like an Egyptian tomb burial, but instead a Minnesotan. She will be ready for any second coming of Christ with extra wool socks tucked away in her coffin.

The subzero temperatures shortened the wake at the church to just an hour. The priest and undertaker wanted to end it earlier, but I insisted we wait at least one hour as someone would likely walk through the door at the last moment, such as my second double cousin the late Charles "Chuck" Walsh (1952–2021). Chuck and I share the same set of Walsh and Foley great-grandparents. This all started when our Walsh grandfathers—brothers—married two Foley sisters, more than a century ago.

Departing the wake, I drove with the parish priest to De Graff Liquor Store to eat dinner, located over three miles west of Murdock on US Highway 12. I actually remember seeing familiar faces, local farmers, but it was just nice to be in a location filled with people, nothing to do with death. Aunt Margaret spent the night in the church in Murdock in the parlor, just off the front entrance. I was hoping she didn't mind the low attendance at her wake, as the church was filled for the funeral, maybe around a hundred or so people; it's really hard to say, as not everyone signs the guest book.

I had arranged Margaret's funeral in 2010 or 2011, when she went to live in the nursing home, recalling how I prepared a check for funeral insurance for Margaret, sat in my car outside the funeral home in Benson, getting up the strength to go inside. I made a selection for the casket, vault, grave stone and more, was escorted around a backroom to see the floor models, making very quick and precise selections. On the day after Margaret's death, I had to confirm my selections, walking through the display models, making the same selections for the second time, with decisions still difficult as the first round of selections a few years earlier.

Margaret's funeral was scheduled for December 7, a Saturday, with the funeral Mass at Scared Hearth Catholic Church in Murdock, followed by burial at Sacred Heart Cemetery. She would travel in the hearse one last time past her home to the cemetery and be placed next to her parents and the rest of her family, already gone from this world.

In the days between Margaret's death and her funeral, with an approaching snowstorm, I divided my time between cleaning out her nursing home room and funeral arrangements. When I arrived back to Margaret's room for the first time after her death, the bed was made perfectly, with white sheets and a cotton blanket, along with a single red rose, and a Gideon's Bible, open to Psalm 23 (NKJV):

The lord is my shepherd; I shall not want.
He makes me to lie down in green pastures;
He leads me beside the still waters.
He restores my soul;
He leads me in the paths of righteousness for His name's sake.
Yea, though I walk through the valley of the shadow of death,
I will fear no evil; for You are with me;
Your rod and Your staff, they comfort me.
You prepare a table before me in the presence of my enemies;
You anoint my head with oil; My cup runs over.
Surely goodness and mercy shall follow me all the days of my life;
and I will dwell in the house of the Lord forever.

There were only a few moments of reflection, as I had my aunt's room to clear out. A snowstorm was forecasted, with no time to spare. I sat for a moment, appearing to be peaceful, then began to tear through the room, creating complete disruption and disorder. The decorated Christmas tree was one of the first items to be removed;

it fit nicely into the large cloth bag in which I originally carried it into the nursing home. The second layer of items I removed included clothing, bedding or blankets requiring dry cleaning, including Margaret's special blue coat from London; it would be going home with me.

As I was sorting out what personal items to keep, donate or discard, a familiar resident was rolled into the room by a staff member to see if the room would be a good fit, featuring a private bathroom, considered to be premium feature. I'm not sure the resident comprehended Margaret died or why the room was available. I was focused on clearing the room, with no time to explain what was really happening. For a year or more, this elderly woman and Margaret had sat next to each other in the dining room next to the window. At one time Margaret was assigned a new spot in the dining room, or as my aunt called it, the restaurant. I had to insist my aunt be returned to the window view, seated next to the same woman who is now looking over Margaret's former room. I'm not sure if they had conversations, but they were each other's company while eating their meals and watching the weather and changing Minnesota seasons.

The day of funeral, December 7, was very difficult and brutal weather, -18 degrees, with a high of -2 degrees. At the time of funeral, 10:30 am, it was -7 with a wind chill of -20. I wore Sorel boots, rated for subzero temperatures, an Irish green cape, worn for the first time, and thermal pants; all this was topped with a blizzard quality down parka I reserve only for severe weather. I walked to the next block from my home to Sacred Heart Catholic Church for the funeral, expecting I'd get a ride with someone to the cemetery, likely from my godfather, the late E. Douglas Larson, known by family as Doug.

During my Aunt Margaret's funeral, the priest made mention of her 1998 white Volvo, a very uncommon car for rural Minnesota, surrounded by Fords. Father's comments about how fast Margaret would drive her car down the road received laughs from the mourners. The reality was she drove very slow, and toward the end of her diving career, about age ninety-three, she was driving on the wrong side of the road to park her car next to the US Post Office, causing great concern; the Postmaster was writing me letters on official stationery. This was combined with a trip each week to Benson for grocery shopping and going to Mass at the Catholic church in Benson, also bringing attention to her shopping and religious practices from local inquisitors.

I know the history of Margaret's Volvo, as I helped her pick it out in late 1997 from a dealership in the Twin Cities, an all-day event. She finally settled on the four-door white Volvo sedan, the first car in her life she had purchased herself. I now own the white Volvo, with just over seventy thousand miles on it. I have the oil changed at a Ford dealership in Atwater, Minnesota. In 2016 I had a carry rack for my kayak installed, a perfect height, as I can keep my kayak on as I drive in to the garage. This is all something Margaret never thought about, and her car is still running and in great condition. About a year ago I was going to sell the Volvo, but it's a car that has so many memories, including the brown paper shopping bags lining the trunk; I finally removed Margaret's walking cane, but left her large umbrella in the backseat, ready to use. I don't feel alone when I'm driving the Volvo, almost like Margaret is with me, but instead my little dog Bobby is in the backseat, covered in an old down jacket in the winter or the windows open in the summer to let fresh air in, as the air conditioning is in need of repairs. I am in love with this car so much, that I'm already thinking if the engine no longer works, I'll have a new one installed. I have a new 2019 Ford, but keep driving Margaret's old Volvo. It's like an old sweater that gets better with age, but there also comes a time for mending.

There are parts of the day from Margaret's funeral I just can't recall, but can remember the chilling Minnesota weather. I recall the priest making the announcement for only the immediate family to go out to the cemetery for Aunt Margaret's burial, and how difficult it was to watch her coffin being wheeled out of the front of the church. The movements at the burial were very quick and precise, with the casket bearers braving -20 degrees wind chill as they lifted Aunt Margaret into place at the gravesite. If the prayers were five minutes, I'd be surprised, likely just an expedited Roman Catholic edition, for which I'm very thankful.

Back to the church basement for lunch, but with prayers said first, as is the custom. As everyone was waiting, I knew people wouldn't eat until the blessing was said, so I led the prayers as no priest was in sight. The ladies at the church prepared hot dishes, sending the leftovers home with me. After my godfather, Uncle Doug, and his sons left me alone at home, it was time to finally rest, something I did for about a week or more, trying to recover from all the events of Margaret's death, cleaning out her room, planning a funeral and just trying to get from one day to the next.

I wear a lot of my aunt's old clothing, many items I purchased during the time Aunt Margaret was in the nursing home, which required all of her things to be labeled, including blankets. There are also the items of my mother's, labeled with her name, including wool socks. I have joked about the times I wear my mother's and aunt's clothing, saying that if I get in an accident and my name is found in my clothing, I'll likely be admitted as Margaret Walsh to a hospital, starting yet another round of the Margaret Walsh confusion. Good thing I wasn't also named Margaret Walsh, but I'd be very proud if I was, as both the Margarets in my life were outstanding women, survivors of the Great Depression and food shortages, who experienced life on the home front during world wars, major changes in society for women, the change of the Roman Catholic Mass from Latin to English, but most importantly, always thinking about ways to make their family's lives better.

Aunt Margaret would write my mother to invite her to meet in Willmar to eat dinner and celebrate holidays. When most people would pick up the phone and make a call, Aunt Margaret sent a very formal invitation to a woman who shared the same name and had known each other for years.

Winter nights, I wear Aunt Margaret's blue wool house coat clearly marked with her name on the belt and embroidered under the collar. In fact I was wearing it last night, keeping warm as I was reading and writing, sitting in the first-floor bedroom at home in Murdock. During the day, I have the white shades drawn up, with white see-through curtains, giving just a little privacy, on the north- and east-facing windows. I replaced the curtains after my return to Minnesota, 2010 or later; it used to be a very heavy drapery with a floral pattern, perhaps a magnolia blossom, with years of service demonstrated with rips and tears, likely dating back to the 1950s or earlier. In the downstairs bedroom, I added a new mattress to the double bed, with the old one likely from the same era as the curtains. Little changes, but the books tucked in the bed's headboard bookcase are the same ones from over the years, including my grandmother's Bible with my birth recorded in it, making the bedroom like a historical museum of family artifacts.

From the hotel down the street on Main Avenue in Murdock, the location of my Aunt Margaret's birth, to the establishment of family headquarters at Main Avenue, I carry on the tradition of living in Murdock. I remember Margaret mentioning in 2009 or so that the house needed to be sold, as she wanted to come live with me in Florida. I'm so happy that I have a place to call home that is filled with history, in a very small wooden house, needing another coat of white paint next summer season.

Although Aunt Margaret is no longer with me alive, there is so much she brought to my life. The only thing I can say is we are still connected with love, something that can't be cut off by death.

In early spring 2014, I paid a visit to Margaret's grave for the first time after winter. The ground was still wet, and the wreath of roses remained, likely because a snowstorm came almost right away after her funeral. As I walked to the grave site to pray, wearing tall rubber boots prepared for any mud, it became obvious I made a mistake; my feet were caught in the mud directly at Margaret's grave, something like quicksand, but just mud, and I wasn't moving and couldn't move my feet, with the suction of the mud and water keeping me engaged in the earth. It went through my mind I'll need to call emergency services, 911, for help, but would need to say I was stuck in the mud of my aunt's gravesite. Trying to work out a better solution, I decided to step out of my boots and jump on the snow, then pull my boots out of the mud. The solution worked, and I walked home with my muddy boots and wet feet. I would wait a month or more before returning to the cemetery, and keep my distance from the fresh graves. Margaret must have had a laugh watching me.

Chapter 10

Irish Passport Stamp

May those who love us, love us
And those who don't love us,
May God turn their hearts.
And if He doesn't turn their hearts,
May He turn their ankles so we'll know
Them by their limping.
—Old Irish saying

May 4, 2018
St. Cloud State University
Herb Brooks National Hockey Center
St. Cloud, Minnesota

LESS THAN A WEEK BEFORE DEPARTING FOR MY fourth trip to Ireland on Friday, May 10, 2018, the entire journey was almost canceled because of a sprained ankle, accompanied by a minor scraped knee and bruised ribs. Most people would cancel a trip under these circumstances, but I continued on as scheduled.

♼

I proudly march out of the spring 2018 commencement with faculty at St. Cloud State University in my academic regalia, complete with my black master's robe with pointed bat-like sleeves, hood of green and white from my alma mater Ohio University, and a black velvet tam and tassel. The sun is hitting the curb and pavement appearing to be one level surface, with no safety indicators to indicate depth changes, about 5 pm out of the Herb Brooks National Hockey Center. I am the faculty representative for the Department of Mass Communications where I teach multimedia, strategic communications, and photojournalism. There is no doubt I look distinguished, maybe even smart, in my robe – right before I fell forward on the pavement. To my left I am flanked by a university librarian, a very resourceful and compassionate person, and remember numerous men offering their hands to help lift me from the pavement. I have great difficulty responding to repeated questions if I was okay as my body, especially my ankle, is now stretched beyond a normal range of motion. The proof was in the pudding, already my right ankle swollen to twice or three times its original size.

Before I know it, I'm now at the St. Cloud Hospital, transported by the librarian and her husband. Hospital registration becomes more of an interrogative interview process located in a closed administrator's office just next to the security check point. A demanding woman insisted on knowing information I felt had nothing to do with my ankle. This reached a point where I was crying.

"You were here in 1982, lived in Mitchell Hall, at St. Cloud State University," said the hospital administer.

"Yes, that's right."

Before I actually saw a doctor, I was rolled in by wheelchair, through hospital security, likely checking for weapons or other contraband.

The trip to the St. Cloud Hospital emergency room revealed the verdict of sprained ankle. The emergency room doctor was quizzing me if I just graduated. His questioning started around what exactly was I wearing during the commencement exercises.

"Were you wearing a velvet hat? How about your colors? What's your university? Did you have a hood? How about your shoes?"

I'm not sure if the reason for the description was just of interest for the doctor to reminisce about his own scholarly regalia, or to build better visual picture in his mind of me falling. It could be more likely he wants to hear the incident in my own words. Medicine is not my area, but I was the patient who limped into the hospital seeking relief and comfort. My greatest concerns pertained to my upcoming trip to Ireland with the emergency room doctor, with responses about walking with crutches and carrying a small backpack. I could not imagine myself in Ireland walking with crutches.

The morning after my injury, I was furious about the possibility of not traveling, making a decision before getting out of bed to continue with my plans for Ireland as scheduled, May 10 to June 5, 2018, twenty-seven days, spending the majority of the visit at a cottage in rural County Kerry near Killarney and a few days in the fair city of Dublin, the capital of Ireland.

My thoughts were focused as such, "If I could only get to Ireland and rest, and let the pain be my travel guide, limiting my walking and activities." Days before my trip were spent at home in Murdock, foot up and still silently fuming about tripping.

Collateral damages thus far after my academically-clad fall include my academic robe needing mending, sprained ankle, bruised ribs and a scraped knee. My turned ankle is noticeable by my slow walking, especially in the first days after my injury. I was determined and ready for international travel, injury and all, not knowing all the obstacles waiting for me, or if I would find new evidence of my family's past in Ireland.

⚜︎

May 10, 2018
Depart 7:30 pm from Minneapolis-St. Paul International Airport

May 11, 2018
Arrive 10:50 am in Amsterdam, the Netherlands
Depart 11:55 am from Amsterdam; arrive in Dublin at 12:35 pm

Just like my unexpected sprained ankle, my travel included detours to Shannon International Airport, Ireland, due to high winds at Dublin Airport coming from the Irish Sea. Aircraft remained parked at the airport for about an hour or more in Shannon, arriving in Dublin about 5 pm, the next day on May 11, 2018, passing through customs and immigration about 5:30 pm. News stories were published about travel problems at Dublin Airport due to high winds.

The day for my travel to Ireland finally arrived on May 10, flying from Minneapolis-St. Paul International Airport to Dublin International Airport, Ireland. My cousin Robert Branshaw, from my mother's family, needed to help me with my bags to the Delta ticket counter in Minneapolis as I struggled, even with my luggage on wheels, from the injuries less than a week prior. I had to take items out of my bags to lighten my load, already experiencing difficulties, but my gate to board my flight was an incredibly short distance, not requiring a wheelchair, as previously expected. "If I could just get to Ireland, I would let my pain be my travel guide." That was my mantra. In the end, I traveled with three bags, one checked for my expedition, the others included a small backpack and small handbag.

I watched about three movies during the Delta flight to Europe, almost unable to sleep, but a few winks between meal services of dinner, breakfast, and refreshments, with more than once, warm moist towels with a hint of citrus were handed out by flight attendants to freshen up in the clouds.

Arrival to Amsterdam was most welcomed, and glad to be back

on solid ground. I had lived in the Netherlands in the late 1990s, and this would be the first time not going beyond the Schiphol Airport to Sittard, a city in Limburg province I once called home. While waiting for my flight to Dublin, I talked with a woman from Den Haag in my limited Dutch about her trip to Dublin to attend her granddaughter's First Holy Communion, serving as an early alert of what I might be encountering in Ireland.

At Schiphol Airport, I joined the other passengers for my flight by taking a bus at the terminal to our aircraft and walked outside in fresh air to climb a staircase into the plane, not a common experience for me as I have almost always embarked via a jet bridge or gangway at airport terminals. After the aircraft departed from Amsterdam to Dublin, I was very exhausted, sleeping almost the entire flight until an announcement by the captain woke me from my much-needed sleep.

The captain announced over the loud speaker system of our unexpected and pending arrival at Shannon Airport due to high winds coming from the Irish Sea at our scheduled airport in Dublin. We would stay parked at the terminal for more than an hour in Shannon before departing for Dublin, arriving about 5 pm

I was saved from massive lines at Dublin Airport, confusion and poor communication, according to an online story by *The Irish Sun*, published on May 11, 2018. Photographs showed travelers in huge crowds, unable to reach their destination as Dublin Airport reported the aircrafts need to take off in the direction of the wind, but unfortunately the direction of the wind was constantly changing, causing the delays. With all this additional information after arriving safely in Dublin, I'm happy I was able to catch up on my sleep at Shannon.

I was very happy to arrive in Dublin after the unexpected travel to Shannon to Dublin, recalling very little about my walk from the arrival gate to Irish customs, but know the distance was short. At Irish customs travelers were sorted by passports a bit like livestock, with lines for European community and non-European community. The wait was also surprisingly quick to present myself at customs. This is also when a litany of questions started by an Irish customs official about all my details, more than I have experienced in all my years of travels.

The process started by me handing over my passport to a gentleman wearing an Irish customs uniform seated behind protective glass, wearing particularly smart looking eye glasses, and epaulets on his shoulders. There was a small opening for me to pass my documents through the window.

The questions started slow, then built up quickly to rapid-fire speed. I was asked to state my business of why I was in Ireland. That was a simple enough question as I responded I was here to see the sights, write, and take photos and videos.

Next came the question about how many days I would be in Ireland, responding with the answer of thirty days, but the actual total days was twenty-six. I'm not sure why I got confused, but caused problems with more questions.

"Do you have a return ticket for your flight home?"

I replied yes and showed him my return ticket and travel itinerary.

"You have poorly planned this trip and you are here thirty days."

There was discussion about how I should have had more paperwork according to the official Irish Immigration site. I was clearly confused at point, thinking I'd be sent home.

"Do you have health insurance?"

I pulled out my health insurance card and handed it over, pointing to the tiny icon of a piece a suitcase meaning travel, something I had researched a few years ago, but didn't seem to satisfy the official.

"You should have followed the directions on our website for your travel as it is thirty days."

If only I could take back my error and correcting to twenty-six days. Surely, this could not be happening.

"Are your accommodations, hotel, paid?"

Yes, I answered and showed my receipts.

"How much money do you have with you?"

I stated how much in US dollars and Euros.

"What are your credit card limits?"

"What other sources of money do you have?"

I answer all the questions as I knew all my resources.

"Where do you work?"

St. Cloud State University, St. Cloud, Minnesota.

"What do you do, teach?"

I'm a professor and teach multimedia and strategic communication.

At this point, the tempo of the questions became almost double or triple fast.

"What are you writing about?"

A manuscript with hopes of becoming a book about my family connections to Ireland, especially Killarney and County Kerry.

"Who will you visit and what are their names? How did you meet?"

I gave names, including a parish priest at Glenflesk, near Killarney.

"What's the title of the book you are writing?"

I gave the working title and the Irish inquisition ceased for a few moments, complete with a large smile.

"When will you complete writing your book?"

Spring 2019 the manuscript will be finished, but the book, I'll have to let you know.

It seemed like I had been standing answering questions in a time warp, longer than I had ever experienced with any customs official in my life.

Finally, I saw behind the thick protective glass the Irish customs official as my luck was decidedly about to change. The left hand and arm moved in a most graceful movement of my Irish inquisitor, almost seeming to be in slow motion before my weary eyes as a stamp was secured in my passport with a loud thump. The nearly bald officer was smiling as he handed back all my documents.

"Welcome to Ireland!"

Finally, I was thinking secretly, not to say anything wrong to restart the questioning.

It was final, and I could enter Ireland, starting to walk to my right, the wrong way, when my new Irish friend started to say something rather important.

"Stop! Miss, you are walking the wrong way. If you continue, you will likely have to answer all the questions again!"

I was thankful and gracious and got myself in the correct direction and out of Irish customs.

Thinking back on this litany of arrival questions, I wonder what part of the Irish customs official was just trying for me to slip on my answers to reveal any hidden or dark plans, such as smuggling out a leprechaun or two in my luggage. I'm certainly glad I didn't say I was looking for leprechauns, pots of gold and fairy forts, but wouldn't mind if I had any chance encounters.

I now have a stamp in my United States of America passport, page nine, stamped in green ink from the Irish Naturalization and Immigration Service, Dublin Airport, 11 May 2018, valid for ninety days for the purpose of a visit.

The day of travel was not over after passing through customs. I hailed a taxi at Dublin Airport, about twenty-five minute ride during high traffic, needing to get to Heuston Irish Rail Station, one of Ireland's main railway stations, and catch the last train of the day to Killarney, about two hundred miles away near the west coast of Ireland. I managed to take the last train from Dublin to Killarney, departing at 6 pm, arriving in Killarney at 10:30 pm. Seated next to me for most of the train travel was a Dubliner who revealed his last name was Walsh, the same as mine; he wasn't willing to share his first name. When the train stopped in Mallow about 8 pm, I changed trains, for the final stage of my long journey since leaving Minnesota the day before, flying over the Atlantic Ocean, riding in a Dublin taxi during rush hour, and arriving in Killarney in the late, dark night.

The train arrived early to Killarney by fifteen minutes, about 10:15 pm, it was dark, and a taxi driver asked if I needed a ride, but said I was waiting for someone to pick me up. I knew this was like at home when the driver said he would wait with me until my ride came as it was dark and the station was unattended. Within moments of my conversation with the taxi driver, Olive Horgan, owner of Crosstown Cottage, arrived with her dear friend Mags O'Sullivan, of Lissivigeen, at the train station to greet me with hugs as if we were old friends.

In about fifteen minutes of travel, Olive transported me back in time, driving on the left side of the road, to Crosstown Cottage, a small stone cottage, estimated to be at least two hundred years old, my home for the next twenty-one days.

After hauling my luggage to the cottage, Olive opened the back door, turned the lights on, the first thing I set my eyes on is an old religious framed painting of the Sacred Heart of Jesus, appearing to be identical to the one in my home in the United States, a very common center piece in Irish homes.

"You must be wrecked," said Olive.

That's Irish slang for you must be exhausted or tired, as I asked her for translation.

The morning would reveal in daylight exactly my surroundings in rural County Kerry. Travel was finally complete, and I would rest safety in the comfort and protection of Crosstown Cottage.

I recall no trouble falling asleep as I was wrecked from international travel.

May 12, 2018
Crosstown Cottage Near Killarney
County Kerry, Ireland

Drive on left. Drive on left. Drive on left. My new chant before driving in Ireland.

I woke up in stone-built Crosstown Cottage in just enough time to eat a bagel and drink a cup of coffee and orange juice before Olive knocked on the back door to the cottage. Today I needed to pick up my rental car at Killarney Airport, located in Farranfore, about fifteen miles from the cottage, all before noon as the rental office is open only a half day on Saturday.

The drive from the cottage was eventful, again needing to become familiar and comfortable with cars driving on the left side of the road, with the driver seated on the right side, nearest the center of the road. This would not be my first adventure driving in Ireland, with first attempts a few years earlier caused me to drive the wrong way in roundabouts at the Shannon Airport, the same airport I rested at the day before. So I practiced driving on farm roads near the airport before venturing on to the Irish roadways.

Olive was concerned I wouldn't find my way back home, offering to wait until my rental car was in hand. Instead I decided to take on the roads, reciting with her like I was preparing for an Olympic event, maybe equestrian or downhill skiing, where to turn, land marks without referring to maps while driving.

The car I received was a diesel-fueled Skoda with automatic transmission, four-door sedan, exact model name was Superb. First, I had never heard of Skoda, a very popular car in Ireland, originating from the Czech Republic. Second, I couldn't start the car, needing to put my foot on the accelerator and turn the key in the ignition. From this car, I would encounter Ireland, maybe discover family history, and very likely get lost.

From Kerry Airport I am traveling south on the N22 to the Cleeney Roundabout, staying on the N22, then right on Lewis Road at roundabout, and right to College Street, finding my way to familiar territory, a Killarney Town car park, or city parking lot, a location I am very familiar with from previous trips.

To celebrate my first Irish travel, about ten miles, I had lunch at Murphy's Bar, located on College Street, just around the corner from the car park, and near the Killarney Courthouse at Fair Hill. Before heading back to Crosstown, I walked to the Killarney town jarvey stand to take a ride on horse and cart, seeking out a familiar jarvey, a jaunting car driver known for wearing an American-style cowboy hat. Tired and my ankle was hurting, I could not resist a ride by horse through the Killarney National Park and Ross Castle.

I drove back to Crosstown Cottage, first stopping at a petrol station to buy diesel on Park Road in Killarney, very close to the town center, as the station is on the left side of the road simply because I was driving on the left side, wanting to keep everything as simplified as possible. Driving back to the cottage, I turned off too early, going to a place called Minish, leaving me wondering if I'd find my way home before dark. Instead of panicking, I pulled out my iPhone and used the Maps app to guide me to the stone cottage.

As far as getting lost, I was more confident than my last trip to Ireland. Surely I'd find my way back to Crosstown Cottage before the Garda Síochána, the Guards, or the Irish Police, needed to be called by Olive looking for an American woman with red hair, and walking with a limp and sprained ankle.

All went well. I made it back to the cottage, drawing deep breaths of relief by myself, and also Olive.

Chapter 11

Bubbling Ḣoly Well
at Shrone City

May 18, 2018
Crosstown Cottage, Crosstown
Killarney, County Kerry, Ireland

IT'S ONE WEEK SINCE I ARRIVED IN IRELAND, NOW sitting in the library loft of the quaint old stone cottage, Crosstown Cottage, my sprained right ankle propped up on a pillow, bruising still noticeable around the right ankle. The width of my right ankle is certainly larger than my left ankle, perhaps even double in size.

The last week allowed for time to rest after transcontinental air travel with my injured ankle; along with finding and buying a pair of larger hiking shoes in Killarney I could adjust to my current ankle situation. In fact, most of my time this past week was spent resting with my foot propped on pillows and chairs, writing in the bedroom just off from the main room in the ground level. The bed and nightstand handily serve as my research desk for maps, notebooks, and Apple MacBook Air laptop computer.

At other times I sit next to one of the windows in the main room of the cottage. The day light illuminates my notebooks through the thick stone wall opening, about the length of my arm. My table while seated at the window was actually the windowsill. In other words, I was doing a lot of writing and research from a brass framed bed and windowsill in an old Irish cottage in Ireland. I was also reaching out to archivists, and other people I had arranged to meet before visiting libraries, museums, and other locations; this trip needed to be even more planned as I would be walking with an injury and driving an automatic transmission car to carry out field research on my family's history.

If I wasn't pursuing writing a book on my family, this trip certainly could have been postponed. My sprained ankle did slow me down, but also allowed to work on my writing, exactly what I came to Ireland to do. Slowing down also savored the new opportunities I had previously planned.

Last night, Thursday, the landlady, Olive Horgan, made a fire in the wood-burning stove as I rested my ankle and wrapped it in a bathroom towel after putting on an ointment for pain and inflammation relief I bought at Sewell's Pharmacy on New Street, downtown Killarney. This was my first experience with an Irish pharmacy. Sewell's has been doing business since 1856, according to the paper bag the store gave me. My own father, during his 1953 trip to Killarney, could have passed by or even visited the same pharmacy for any of his ailments during travel.

Seated next to the wood burning stove, Olive insists on looking at my foot to see if it was starting to heal.

"You must have good healing for your body to make such a noticeable change," said Olive. She was right, as the day I arrived in Ireland, my ankle was more swollen than today.

Next, I mention to Olive about the holy well at Shrone I visited on Wednesday (May 16, 2018), attempting to get any additional help for my sprained ankle, dipping my fingers in the well and making the sign of cross. Shrone, Shrone City, or simply the City by local residents, is located in rural County Kerry, about four miles east of the village of Barraduff on the N72 road, near Killarney. The modern-day name of the City comes from Cathair, an Irish word for Stone Fort or Castle, and believed this site was a place of pilgrimage and one of the first sites in Ireland to be populated, with ongoing excavations, according to historical information signs on location. The site is referenced among one of the western world's oldest center of worship and celebration, a site of Ireland's transition from paganism to Christianity. Shrone's holy well was once associated with pagan spirituality, and today a source of Christian Holy Water and healing.

While traveling on the N72 road east from Killarney to Barraduff, it is easy to miss the turnoff, but there's a white sign marked Shrone, three kilometers, pointing the way down a one-track road. Drivers need to be prepared to give way to farm tractors, and to back up to allow other cars to pass. The last part of the road just before arriving in Shrone, dips down and winds and turns even more, passing through a farmer's land, and grazing dairy cattle, depending on the time of day. Arriving at Shrone, I find there is no city, at least presently.

As Olive wasn't familiar with Shrone, I shared with her directions. I've somehow committed the directions to memory as I've been lost several times attempting to go there. I first visited Shrone in 2011, as it's just a few miles away from Townland Knockanarroor, a location associated with a family baptismal record.

Shrone, located in the foothills of the Paps Mountains or the Paps of Anu, are two nearly identical shaped round mountains, often referenced an outline of a woman's bosom while accompanied with a smile, with prehistoric cairns, man-made piles or stacks of stone. According to historical signs at Shrone, the mountains and the pre-Christian religious site is associated with Anu, the Mother Goddess, and the cairns, likely date to the Neolithic or Bronze age. Religious practices dating back four thousand years or more, is situated in the ruins of a stone circle fort. According to Celtic spirituality, the City is a penitential station, a place to pray for local peasants performing rounds, or paying rounds, an earlier system of forgiveness for absolution before the introduction of the Sacrament of Penance, or confession, during the early centuries of Christianity. Area residents drove their cattle to drink from the holy well on the west side of the site, according to the late author and folklorist Dan Cronin, *In the Shadow of the Paps.* Cronin spent his life surrounded by the Paps collecting stories and local folklore. Local faithful walked to marked locations of stones or beds and prayed for forgiveness.

During the twentieth century, Shrone became home to Christians and festivities on May Day. In recent years, visitors come in May to pray the Rosary as they walk clockwise inside and outside the cashel, or stone fort wall. Visitors are free to visit all year round, but first they must find their way along winding country roads to Shrone.

Cronin writes of an elaborate eleven-step process for praying at Shrone, called the Rounds, as told to him by an elderly resident. This involves walking and praying at certain locations inside the stone fort circle, a location considered a hallowed sanctuary in Ireland. One of the steps involves tracing a cross inside a circle, known as a Celtic Cross, on stones at the old megalithic altar in the stone fort. The final step of the rounds includes praying at the holy well, and pilgrims are encouraged to drink from the well, or take the holy water home.

⚜️

Today, about 4 pm, I've decided to return to Shrone and seek yet another healing for my sprained ankle. Unlike my last visit today my plan is to dip my entire sprained ankle into the holy well. Packing a few tea towels from the kitchen, camera gear and notebooks, I'm driving to the remote and sacred holy well in the foothills of the Paps. My original plan for this trip was to walk up one of the mountains of the Paps, in fact had already contacted local outdoor experts, but I'll need to settle for soaking my ankle in a holy well.

After driving through the winding roads to Shrone, located in Townland Gortnagane, I park my car as close as possible to the entrance of the walled fort near the south of the stone enclosure, just off the road to allow cars, and especially farm tractors to pass on the dirt road.

Using my set of hiking poles, I walk through the center of the freshly cut carpet of grass in the open air fort, passing by the megaliths in the center, a shed, and the remains of a small stone cottage with a rusted metal roof, once inhabited by a caretaker, a *deerhough*, of the holy well.

Walking down a path of steps to the well, between the shed and cottage, it is here I've come to seek a cure for what is ailing me, a sprained ankle. The well is surrounded by a wall of field stones, and abandoned ceramic tea and coffee cups for drinking the holy water are randomly resting on the stone wall. There are ribbons and strips of cloth tied to vegetation growing on the interior of the wall associated with prayers and blessings of St. Brigid of Kildare, a patron saint of Ireland, all in the hopes of bringing healing. If I look back toward the south, I can see a view of the Paps Mountains.

Sitting on the concrete floor next to the well, I remove my sock, shoe and special ankle support from my right foot, feeling the chill of the holy well's water, with about a two feet high metal basin off the ground. I let out a loud a loud "Oh!" as my foot touches water, birds are chirping, and wind is noticeable in this tiny open enclosure. Next, I make the sign of the cross.

Now, I am silent, thinking if soaking my foot in this holy well will make my ankle free of pain, it has not yet happened, as there is still obvious bruising, and pain. Next, I pray the Our Father once, followed by one Hail Mary, doing a bit of a freestyle praying of the rounds, finishing with another sign of the cross.

I am in no physical condition do the full round of prayers traditional for Shrone, and my foot and leg are still dunked in the well. The water from the well likely is coming from the small stream running off from the Paps. If the water table is high, the water appears to be bubbling. Today there is slight movement, though unsure I see bubbles, except around my feet. Now a minute or two more, my foot is feeling relaxed, pain is lessened a bit, as the cool mountain spring is giving relief, if only temporary. Feeling I've had enough of the holy well, about two minutes appearing to be my limit, I hoist my leg out of the water, and use the tea towel to wipe off the remaining holy well water on my foot.

After finishing up at the holy well, I walk to the center of the fort, near the megalith stones. Here I stand almost in the center of a stone fort. To the west is Knockanarroor and Killarney, not far from where my family lived. Standing here, the foothills and the Paps meet with the land, sky and heavens. Ancient ruins are surrounding me. I am completely alone, not a person in sight, yet I feel completely at home.

Looking to the west, rays of sun pass through the sky, creating dramatic diagonal rays of white light falling above my view of the old cottage. Shining through the dark clouds are glimpses of pink and blue lights in the horizon as sunset approaches in the west back toward Killarney. Here I stand, looking around in all directions in a vantage point of reaching with my outstretched arms to touch heaven, or so I think. The landscape lends itself as an outside natural cathedral or basilica resting in nature, grander than any man-made dwelling.

There is thinking of the ancient Celts of places where reality is not the same as everywhere else, referring to "thin places," according to the late author Patricia Monaghan, *The Encyclopedia of Celtic Mythology and Folklore*. Thin places might be where the otherworld is nearby, including dwellings of fairies in trees, or underground in nearby Paps.

Personally, I think Shrone is included in the thin places, similar to my view of the edge of my world at home in Murdock at sunset when the sky is painted colors that hypnotize all my thoughts, especially of my departed family.

Back in my car, slowly making my descent down from Shrone, passing through a farm yard, a herd of about fifty Friesian black and white milk cows parade home to their barn for their evening milking with hooves clomping, loud mooing and bags full of milk after a day of eating grass. A black and white border collie and its farmer makes sure all the ladies make it home safe to the cow shed. These beasts historically received their own blessings on May Day at Shrone; it seems appropriate I am greeted by cows as I depart Shrone.

ॐ

Now back in the safety of Crosstown Cottage, about 10 pm, eating a late evening meal and resting from my travel to Shrone, I am not sure of any miraculous changes in my foot and ankle, but at least I tried my luck at the ancient Irish holy well.

The healings could be in the cool mountain water in the holy well, although temporary.

The healings could be where land and sky appear to be very close, with heaven only the distance of my outstretched arms.

The healing could be how my soul feels free on the same ground pilgrims before me sought hope and comfort from daily struggles.

I wanted to climb the Paps on this trip in order to see first-hand the panoramic views, but instead, I connected in the same way Irish have done for millennia before me at Shrone—through the sacred and hallowed ground and through prayer. This is the experience when science stops, faith steps in, and when all else fails, faith is the only guide.

Chapter 12

Irish Crosstown Cottage

May 20, 2018
Crosstown Cottage, Crosstown
Killarney, County Kerry, Ireland

I OPEN A WOODEN GATE WITH A METAL LATCH, AND carefully watch my steps down a small, stoned path connecting Crosstown Cottage and Stone Arch House. I've been invited to an evening meal with my Irish hosts, Olive and John Horgan and their family.

Walking just steps away, I arrive next door from Crosstown Cottage, standing at the front entrance to Stone Arch House, push the electric doorbell button but also use the large round metal door knocker with a figure of a lion. Besides knocking with the novelty, I am unsure if the bell worked, as the bell chimes are silent to me as a visitor. Back home in Murdock, I don't even have a door bell on my house, so visitors just need to knock loudly. Olive greets me at the door saying she needs to go shopping and get a few items at Daly's, a grocery store in Killarney, and asks if I'd like to join her. Of course, I said yes. It is all typical not to have everything you need for a meal, and adding an adventure with Olive is certainly in on my list.

I jump in the front passenger seat, left side in Ireland, and Olive drives her brown sport utility vehicle toward Killarney, arriving at Daly's on Park Road, a short distance from the center of town. Parking at the grocery store requires expertise, as parking is tight, much less spacing between cars than I am familiar with back in the States. Olive backs into an open parking space near the front entrance with the ease of experienced and accomplished Irish driver. I would have simply found another parking spot, or even circled around until the ultimate parking opportunity was presented, or moved on to another store.

The mission of this grocery store run is hunting and gathering an apple tart, known to most Americans as simply apple pie, whipped cream, and ice cream, no other translations needed. Within minutes of entering Daly's, Olive is greeted by numerous friends, all with short conversations asking about their families while picking up shopping baskets near the entrance.

One of the many ladies immediately says to me, "Oh, I know all about you."

With that, I replied, "I hope it's all good!" I didn't have anything to hide, and the encounter was delightful, as are all of Olive's friends I'm meeting.

Shoppers walk past me, knowing exactly where to find their favorite Irish Brennan sandwich breads and other groceries, but I'm operating at tourist visa level in this grocery store, although it's not my first Irish grocery store. The thinking of a customer applies when you shop at a familiar grocery store back home in the States, and you know where to find your favorites items; in this case, however, Olive is taking the lead. From my view standing near the oranges, lemons, and other fruits and vegetables, I see a gentleman walking out of my line of sight to the left, carrying in his left hand a smart phone and a metal wire basket with red handles, heading toward a display of meats near the deli section. Walking in the opposite direction is a woman pulling a small red basket equipped with wheels and a pull handle, part basket and shopping trolly filled with groceries, topped with a frozen pepperoni pizza. This little pull cart and basket intrigued me, and I chat briefly with the shopper, who, not surprisingly, is known by Olive. Just to the left of me is a display of Daly's Killarney Apple Tarts covered in a transparent protective wrap, weighing in at almost one and half pounds. I now understand why this apple tart, with a dusting of sugar on the crust was sought after – it's a huge pie, a perfect mix of butter, flour, sugar, apple, margarine, and eggs.

Heading back to Crosstown, Olive and I realize we forgot the most import item from the grocery store, ice cream, but there is no turning back. I start to think about how Olive makes me feel as part of her family. She has welcomed me into her cottage, home and family, and ultimately is giving me a deeper look into Irish culture, something that cannot be done staying in a hotel. My sprained ankle limits me getting around and requires extra rest, but has helped enrich my understanding of the Irish people on a personal level as I'm walking around at slower than turtle speed.

It was a bit of mistake or chance I came to stay at the Horgan's cottage. It was my plan to stay at a hotel in Killarney on College Street as I know that area of town from previous trips to Ireland. When I prepared to book a room, in about the time of just a day or so, all the rooms were booked because of the Killarney horse races a few days after my arrival, and tourists coming from around the world and also wanting to see the famous Lakes of Killarney, Killarney National Park, Gap of Dunloe, and a short distance to Cobh, an Irish seaport. So, in searching for alternative accommodations was the incredible surprise of Crosstown Cottage, situated in the rural countryside. It also afforded an opportunity to go deeper into Irish culture, along with shopping and eating Irish Apple Tarts.

Olive is originally from County Tipperary, famous for the Rock of Cashel, and the song "It's a Long Way to Tipperary," made famous by marching solders during the First World War. She married a Kerry man, as she says, a man from County Kerry named John Horgan. During this time, she was working at a hotel in Killarney. She now works at a local school. The couple has three boys, Darren, twenty-two, Johnaton, nineteen, and Kieran, ten, ages as of May 2018.

After the Daly's grocery trip, Olive and I are welcomed back to Stone Arch House with the aroma of bacon cooking as John is the evening's top chef. This bacon is more in appearance to sliced ham, leaner than the American version of bacon, closer to resembling Canadian bacon or a cooked ham. An Irish dish I am not familiar with, Colcannon, pronounced coal-cannon, made of mashed potatoes and cabbage, is being prepared by John, along with homemade parsnip sauce, a creamy white sauce, and side dish of carrots.

Daylight is flowing in through the kitchen window next to the sink and stove, and white dinner plates are being prepared, first with bacon, followed by colcannon and carrots topped with parsley sauce. Parsley sauce in a small sauce pan is poured directly from the stovetop over the bacon and colcannon. John asks his youngest son Kieran if he wants parsley sauce with his meal, receiving a reply he wants only just the tiniest bit. Just a few feet away from John at foot level is Molly, a black-and-tan King Charles spaniel, wagging her tail, waiting for any handouts or food to drop her way, especially bacon.

Now ready to eat, a blessing is prayed as we are seated in the dining room just off the kitchen. The Horgans tell me they are fast eaters, and they prove it, but the speed can't be rated or compared, as I am an extra slow eater, talking too much and asking questions during the meal about this, that, and so many other things Irish.

After dinner, I played a few rounds of Pokeman with Kieran on his Nintendo Switch computer game. It was my first experience with this game, with no idea what was happening with the monsters and balls of fire, although I won at least one round before retiring from the game.

Next, as I appear now to be the honored guest from America warranting a concert, I am serenaded with music by Kieran's Irish whistle, sometimes called a tin whistle and penny whistle. Killarney is known for making the famous Killarney Whistle, and is a vertical six-holed instrument, similar to a recorder, often associated with Irish music, and also considered a great way to learn music.

Kieran opens his handwritten music notebook complete with notes for playing his whistle, but not sheet music, using the dining room table as his music stand as the remaining cups and plates are being removed for washing up. Holding the nickeled-plated whistle in his two hands, the young whistler starts playing after his mother gives him an okay to begin an Irish air, a slower piece, called "Eamon an Chnoic," also known as "Ned on the Hill," a somber ballad. Then he asks if I'm ready for his next song, and Olive introduces a lively jig, "Johnny Leary's Jig."

"Very good, Kieran," says Olive, while receiving a round of applause from his family and myself after he finishes his song.

Moving back into the kitchen, Olive prepares coffee as I sit in the kitchen and continue to ask questions and talk with family. The oldest Horgan son, Darren, offers to play one of his own compositions on the piano from memory near the living room, while sounds of dishes and cleaning up in the kitchen commences. Darren is a talented young composer and musician, with aspirations of a career in music. Missing from the musical evening presentations is middle son, Johnaton, still away at college for the last semester of the academic year, a talented Irish dancer, competing at world-class championship levels.

During this visit with the Horgans, I am hoping to learn more about their cottage and their rural neighborhood. John talks to me about Mangerton Mountain that can be viewed from their house and cottage. Standing outside looking west, the horizon is implied as it breaks the line where the sky meets the outline of the mountains. From this perspective looking west toward Killarney town, Stone Arch House is in the foreground to my left, and there is a row of modern homes in the cluster or settlement, all appearing to be built in recent years, except for Crosstown Cottage.

The wood fence and gate separate Crosstown Cottage and Stone Arch House physically, and about two hundred years or more of time. The actual age of the cottage is unknown, though it is estimated to have been built around 1818, before the Great Famine, 1845–1852. It was refurbished by John, taking about two years to complete in the early 2000s. The Horgans' new home, Stone Arch House, was built in 2006 and came complete with the dilapidated artifact and ruins called Crosstown Cottage.

Crosstown Cottage is situated in rural Townland Crosstown, with an Irish name of Gort na gCros, pronounced Gort na gross, meaning cross or crossroads and fields, just a short distance east of Killarney town. Many Irish places take their names after the land and its surroundings. Crosstown takes its name more specifically from its location on the map and the crossroads between two major roads east of Killarney, referenced as the Cork Road, or road to Cork (N22), a road from Killarney to Cork; and Mallow Road or road to Mallow (N72), a road from Killarney to Mallow. The confusion comes for tourists, including me, because the roads are marked with numbers on maps, not Cork Road and Mallow Road, as local residents reference the roads in the direction of travel, requiring another level of confusion. The Cork Road and a portion of the Mallow Road are part of the ancient Butter Roads, old routes used by farmers to carry their butter by horse and cart to the Butter Exchange in Cork, where it was sold and shipped out of Ireland. County Kerry's butter is high in fat as the cows graze on the lush grasses, helping to preserve butter during transportation. It's highly likely butter produced at Crosstown Cottage was also shipped abroad from Cork.

There's no center of commerce in Crosstown. It's more a cluster or settlement of homes with a road referenced as Crosstown, but is actually a road without a name, lined with homes and farms expediting travel, sometimes narrowing to a one-lane road. Landmarks are needed to know where to turn, and local knowledge is required for car travel. GPS can help but driving with eyes on the road is required. There are points on the winding road to Crosstown Cottage wrapping around ancient houses and barns that appear to be located in the middle of the road. Drivers of cars or trucks must yield to approaching cars, pulling to the side of road, often allowing for only one car at a time, while cars and farmers' tractors pass with care, almost always waving at fellow motorists. A local Irish storyteller, or *seanchaí* in Irish, sounds like shawnakee, once lived down this winding road near the cottage, according to Olive.

John certainly spent a great deal of time restoring his old cottage, in fact he now restores cottages as a business, along with his other sought-after skills, such a metal work, as many local residents need his knowledge, a lot of it related to and learned at Crosstown Cottage. When asked about what he thinks about his cottage, he replied, "I love it. Never spent a night in it."

The cottage's floor plan measures only twenty by thirty-eight feet, with the roof apex about twenty feet. It has a second-floor loft for sleeping, with heating provided by a multifuel stove capable of burning wood, wood pellets or peat, along with a modern secondary heating source. The foundation is made of field stones, and the walls are made of limestone, with a thickness of about an arm's length—three to four feet wide. In the hallway at Stone Arch House, a photograph display shows the stages of renovation of the formerly dilapidated structure, not inhabited since the 1980s by a Dutch man when there was an extension or lean-to attached to the cottage, and modern tin roof covering an old, thatched roof. A surveyor's bench mark was discovered during the renovation, looking like a crow's foot, but unfortunately was inadvertently covered over by plaster during restoration.

According to the 1853 Griffith's Valuation, an important Irish genealogical source, the owner of Crosstown Townland was the Reverend B. Herbert, a principal lessor of the parish of Killaha. Herbert is part of the same family at Muckross House, located in the most beautiful locations, Killarney National Park. During 1853, there were at least three houses in Crosstown Townland with the family names of Connors, McGillycuddy, and Leary. It is unknown if the present-day cottage in Crosstown is one of the houses listed, but the location cannot be far away, if it is not the very same location.

Additional details I found about Crosstown Townland come from the National Archives of Ireland 1901 and 1911 census. In 1901, twenty people lived in Crosstown with the family names of Connor, Culloty, Dinneen, and Hogan, all Roman Catholic, and were listed by relationship to the farmer, such as farmer's wife, farmer's son, scholar and one servant boy, including their literacy and ages. In 1911, the census had listed only fifteen people living in Crosstown, with three houses. It is unknown if there were residents of Crosstown Cottage in 1911, as there are no house numbers, road names, as there are none today, simply Crosstown Cottage. There is no need to worry about a house number if you are sending mail as the Crosstown Cottage is the address, the same today as for past residents, a customary practice in rural Irish countryside.

The perspective from the front of the cottage shows a view looking east. Standing at the green painted forged iron gate, is a wall of whitewashed stone, very common from the Great Famine period. Growing on the whitewashed stone wall are small pink flowers called Herb Robert, *Geranium robertianum*. The tiny flowers with red stems are attached to the stones, and could have been used by residents for treating aliments by drinking as a tea. As pretty as the pink flower appears, it can be a stinky plant. There is a grace and setting of the land, marked with the stone wall; likely it once completely surrounded the property in a courtyard farmyard layout, common in Ireland. Ruins of the stone barn still remain, once part of the walled property, just two or maybe three feet from the stone wall to the dotted yellow line of the paved road in front of Crosstown. The elevation of the road pitches a short distance to the north from the barn, making for difficult and dangerous locations for both drivers and pedestrians.

Walking through the green gate in front of Crosstown Cottage is a paved walkway to the front door, with a front yard of grass. I tried walking on the grass, going only a few steps before sinking in the boggy lawn before realizing the lawn is more for display. In the past farmers might have kept livestock in the courtyard. A tall green hedge, most likely a Myrtus hedge, creates a boundary next to the ruins of the barn, reaching high or higher than the roof of the cottage. If the timing is just right, the hedge will cast a jagged shadow against the stone wall as the sun falls in the evening. There are the remains of an old bicycle, fifty or more years old, adding to the charm of the cottage. Although several years have passed since it transported passengers, it's a great photo opportunity.

Three windows have a Kelly-green trim, two on one side, and a door almost directly situated in the front of the cottage. The windowsills and roof line are trimmed in white, making the white lace curtains stand out with flowers in the terracotta colored window boxes. Built in a traditional Kerry style, this cottage has the typical qualities of a long and narrow structure with small windows. Originally, there was no back door, only a front door, with the hearth or fireplace in the middle for burning turf or wood for cooking and heating, and a tiny window on the back side of the house. Earliest residents in the 1880s likely slept near the fireplace and in lofts, or with beds that could be folded away in a box during the day, or a bed with frame and curtains for privacy.

The roof is now made of corrugated tin painted in green, but it was formerly thatched. When the Horgan family started renovations, an original thatched roof was found under a former tin roof. Today the cottage has a modern tin roof with a wood lined ceiling. The elevation is 310 feet above sea level, not likely to flood unless another Ice Age comes, or the Irish Sea comes inland, many years in the future, if it would happen at all as a result of global warming.

I usually enter the cottage from the back door that was added during the twenty-first century. What a wonder it might have been for the original occupants to have more than one door to enter, and something that is certainly taken for granted today.

❧

Cottages in County Kerry, and throughout Ireland, often kept livestock inside the same dwelling as the family. Crosstown Cottage lacks written history, but it is possible in the earlier years that one edge or corner of the home served as a corral or cowshed called a byre, sounds like buyer. The byre dwelling might have had a separation between the living quarters, such as a wall, but some form of drain for waste from the animals and food and hay stored inside the cottage on a loft, similar to historic period cottages I visited at Muckross Traditional Farms in Killarney, and more in Ireland. In the case of Crosstown Cottage, if there was a byre, the logical location was on the south edge of the house as the elevation appears to be the lowest, as situated on the land. This location might be the same as the present-day sitting room or kitchen on the ground floor. If the walls could speak, this small mystery could be solved. Did another home once stand in the location of the present cottage? What is true is that Irish farmers built their homes based on material available for the region, in this case field stones, especially limestone. As more buildings were added, like a barn apart from the dwelling for humans, the layout changed for the cottage, with bedrooms, fireplace, kitchen, and sleeping area.

Crosstown Cottage once had a stone lean-to attached to an outer wall but was removed during renovation in the early 2000s. The structure could have served as an extra bedroom, storeroom, or place to keep animals. There are two lofts for sleeping in the cottage, one located over the kitchen and bathroom, and the other bedroom. The roof is low in the loft, so you need to watch your head. Standing in the loft I have only have a few inches to spare before hitting my head on the ceiling; it is only about six feet from the floor of the loft to ceiling. The stone walls of the old cottage do not talk, but historical evidence in County Kerry helps to piece back time, but that exact order is unknown.

I asked Olive if she thought animals once lived in her cottage. "Oh, God yes! If you had a prize pig, you would mind it like a human as it was your livelihood."

On a visit to the cemetery in Listry Townland in search of my family roots, Olive drove and guided me along the countryside, Saturday. There was a strong smell of manure blowing toward the graveyard and church. "It's the smell of heather," said Olive, in typical Irish wit. "If you would bottle that good old Irish smell, you could sell it to the Americans twenty times over. It smells like home."

"It's what people smelled years ago and when the animals slept in the houses."

Olive was exactly right about the smell of home, but I'm not sure if this particular smell would be a hit. Today at home in Murdock, if the wind is blowing in the wrong direction, I can catch a hint of the same bovine smell from area dairy farms when I walk outside my house. This smell can also be called the smell of money as it's associated with dairy products and honest hard work.

Crosstown Cottage today has modern conveniences with running water, flush toilet, shower, electricity, a working fuel stove for turf or wood for heating along with central heating, a small refrigerator, and fuel stove for cooking. I washed dishes with Fairy Soap, a popular brand of soap in Ireland, in the old white farm sink in the cottage, putting cups and plates back in the open cupboards at the end of the day. I flipped switches to turn on the burners for the stove, scrambling eggs and frying bacon, seeming to cook too fast or to slow, as I was trying to get a grasp of the foreign stove. Dish towels were placed to dry next to the sink, or maybe over the handle of a door. A little refrigerator kept brown bread fresh, and my other provisions cold. In the little cottage I was safe, and was at home. In my notebooks, I made rough sketches of the layout and floor plans of Crosstown Cottage with doors, kitchen, sitting room, bedrooms, all not to scale, but for me to remember, and know this Irish cottage after my bags are packed, and I am at home again in Minnesota.

What made this tiny cottage home? There's old world charm with the antique plates, six in total, lining the entrance to the kitchen, mounted to the large wooden beam to the library loft directly above the kitchen and bath. A feather duster and broom hang on the wall under a small section of the loft, near the staircase, but more like a ladder, as it steep. Walking up to the library loft in a ladder-style staircase, I make sure I hold on to the side railing. There are shelves lined with books, old and new, including *Butler's Lives of the Fathers, Martyrs and other Saints*, very appropriate for an Irish cottage. Included in the mini library area are kettles and tea pots, perhaps Spanish. A ceiling window opens with a grand view of the Mangerton Mountains, along with sounds of cars passing on the road, and Molly, the Horgan's dog, barking to catch some attention. Birds can be heard chirping away, while cows moo at a nearby farmyard. As I stick my head out the ceiling window, I see about a dozen modern homes near Crosstown Cottage.

Looking down into the sitting room from the library loft, I can see the modern heating stove, located almost in the center of the cottage. A rustic chandelier with candle sticks hangs with modern electrical lighting. Copper pots, about seven, a soup ladle and other items add charm for cooking, but are just for decoration.

At this point I go back down to the ground floor and climb up to the sleeping loft with two single beds, tucked under the roof so there is just enough room to stand in the middle of the floor, trying not to hit my head. Midmorning light is flowing in and casting light on the floor near the beds. After making the climb on the staircase next to the fireplace, I look back to the open first floor, with the large Sacred Heart of Jesus, old and weathered, the first item I noticed when I arrived at the cottage.

After I finish my visit to the sleeping loft, I descend to the sitting room. There is a crucifix placed above the hearth, attached to the support beams for the sleeping loft.

Trying to figure out exactly what has happened in Crosstown Cottage is difficult, let alone assemble a list of former residents with existing Irish census records. Better yet, why do I care about the human habitation? I think to know a home, knowing the people that lived here, help to tell a more complete story of the stone cottage.

What is likely, inhabitants witnessed all that is great in life, and also that is miserable, including the Great Famine, and other periods of food scarcity. Deaths, births, conceptions all took place under the roof of Crosstown Cottage. The smell of peat, also known as turf, for cooking and heating can still be smelled today. Constant prayers, especially the Rosary of Hail Marys, in Irish and English, pleaded for speedy recovery from ailments, or peaceful deaths. Residents practiced their Catholic faith in private or secret during the Penal Years, and traveled to nearby locations for Mass celebrated on rocks, far out of the eyes of the ruling English class. Babies born, living a full life or few hours, followed by mothers dying after giving birth. Multiple generations under one roof, along with horses or other livestock for safe keeping and to warm the cottage during long winter months. Being turned out for no good reason by the landlord, unable to make payment to landlord. In this cottage people might have said their last good words, or no words at all, before emigrating to North America or other locations, to ensure life for generations to follow.

May 28, 2018
Crosstown Cottage, Crosstown, Killarney
County Kerry, Ireland

In the evening, just after 7 pm, Molly barks while birds sing, and cars pass in front of the cottage. I walk still with my hobble out to the edge of the road, outside of the white-washed stone wall, with the green painted iron gate. Now I hear the clomping of horses' hooves from two horseback riders on a Connemara and Welsh horse, and another on an Irish Sport horse tromping past the green iron gate with whitewash stone wall board at Crosstown Cottage before I venture out on a walking tour.

After chatting with the equestrians for a few minutes, I start my walk less than a few blocks the cottage, to the hill with the Ogham stone, pronunciations are oh-hum or ogg-em, a standing stone with a primitive Irish alphabet set in a linear form, in a nearby farmer's cow pasture dating back about five thousand years. My sprained ankle will allow me to be only a spectator as the walk up the hill is just beyond my current abilities.

Arriving at the hill, I watch from the road as a local farmer moves his cattle around the hill with Ogham stone. I was so close to the Ogham stone, yet so far from touching history and see the primitive writings in person, something to save for another trip to Ireland.

The stroll back to the cottage, the distance of two blocks, includes passing by oxeye daisies growing wild along the road. It became clear that I was on the correct path when I could see the farmer high up on the hill, appearing to be more of a flat surface like a table or plateau, covered with a carpeting of green grass and cattle, with peaks of Mangerton in the distance. The narrow road I walk on appears almost to be a half circle with houses surrounding, permitting just one car to pass at a time, so I needed to pay attention to traffic while taking in the view.

I cherish my brief conversation with the busy farmer after he walked down from his hill on this lovely Irish night in Crosstown, as the shadows of trees cast on the narrow road, and I returned to the cottage. From this conversation what is most significant, although short, about a childhood memory of Crosstown Cottage, "I remember this open place as a child."

Here by the daisies, I chatted with a man walking his dog to make sure I was on the correct unmarked road, as most roads are unmarked in this Irish countryside.

Certainly, this beautiful moment will stay in my mind, with the Mangerton Mountain setting the movie scene for my daydream. I'll be experienced with the rural countryside of with Crosstown

Cottage, a tiny stone cottage I called home for twenty-one days with charm and wisdom of neighbors, tutored in Irish culture and modern-day life.

♨️

History of the land of Ireland includes Crosstown Cottage and surroundings on the local scale, bearing witness to Stone Age farmers, with an Ogham Stone, estimated five thousand years old.

Two thousand years ago Jesus was walking the earth in a location we call the Holy Lands. About four thousand miles away to the west in Crosstown, inhabitants would be looking toward Mangerton Mountains, likely the same as I am today, watching as the last light of day leaves the sky at the end of the day.

St. Patrick, St. Brigid of Kildare, St. Colman, along with numerous other Irish saints, were busy traveling across Ireland, baptizing, and spreading Christianity. Vikings, Normans, and Black Death all made a mark on the island and the Irish race. Ireland has endured during the modern era, political and religious persecutions by the British, along with the Great Famine starting in 1845, the 1916 Easter Rising, the Michael Collins assassination in 1922 and Irish Troubles lasting thirty years starting in the 1960s. There are intense conversations raging of the possibility of Ireland as one country, but the outcome remains to be seen in the future. In 2020, Crosstown Cottage added a global pandemic to its history, as people around the globe took refuge in their homes, and the world as we knew it stood still.

♨️

In the back garden of Crosstown Cottage is an old ash tree with a fairy garden and a protective wooden deck and fence. Large rocks the size of fists are situated around the base of the tree. On the tree's trunk are numerous manmade tiny doors about the size of an adult human hand, apparently just the right size of local fairies to enter, along with a string of outdoor lights for evening fairy parties. This ash is a large and graceful tree, providing shade, yet its base provided a dramatic view of its root system reaching down into the boggy landscape. Some mythology related to the oak tree is that it wards off fairies and guards against evil. This tree is more of a welcoming bed and breakfast for fairies with all the fairy doors attached to the trunk.

Olive told me she decorated the tree with the help of her family, adding another level of Irish folklore to the cottage. Whether any fairies have been identified at this tree is unknown, but trees and fairies are integrated into Irish culture, for fairy believers and fairy nonbelievers alike.

Trees, along with fairies, play an important role in Irish folklore, with all tree species having potential mystical qualities, including hawthorn, oak, and ash. Cutting down a known fairy tree can bring about misfortune, and this belief in fairy trees is still alive in modern times in Ireland.

✌

Michael Lynch, archivist at the Kerry Library in Tralee, County Kerry, shared with me as a general issue, the superstitions, including stories around changelings, babies or small children thought to be completely controlled by fairies, also referred to as fairy children, which was very common in Ireland. This is reflected in the stories found in the Irish Folklore Commission in their national survey of the 1930s.

Just less than two miles away from Crosstown Cottage, the Flesk River flows. A fairy-related murder was reported in the Flesk of a young boy thought to be possessed by fairies in 1826, according to Freeman's Journal, July 28, 1826, Dublin. The exact location of the misfortune along the Flesk is unknown, but details include an elderly woman named Ann Roche, indicted for the murder of Michael Leahy, age four. The young boy was unable to stand, walk or speak, and thought to be fairy struck, a folklore idea of someone losing use of one's body, and a punishment for offending fairies. A cure of bathing the young boy in the Flesk went on for three days, with him drowning on the final day. A witness during cross-examination during the trial said what happened was not to kill the child, but "to put the fairy out of it." A jury gave the verdict of not guilty. It could be the jury believed in fairy children, as it was common for the period, and had no intention of offending fairies, and meet with any misfortune.

✌

On a more angelic folk culture note, next door to Crosstown Cottage at Stone Arch House is a tiny yellow door with a daisy and a round arch almost five inches tall. This fairy door is situated on the white baseboard, in direct contact to the wood floor, making for easy access to a resident fairy named Ferno. The fairy arrived in 2016 and makes occasional appearances, leaving tiny notes for Kieran, but the actual fairy has not been seen. Food, such as biscuits or sweets, have been left with notes to attract Ferno from behind the fairy door, but encounters with Molly, the Horgans' dog, have likely sabotaged fairy and human relations, eating food before the fairy had a chance to retrieve gifts. Irish fairies, from my understanding, handle more than the regular tooth fairy duties, enjoying year-round activities, and tiny letter writing with their host families in Ireland. There's even a magic key that's put out in a tiny bottle usually at night. If the key is missing in the morning, it a sure sign a fairy visited, or Molly has hidden the key.

I am so impressed with the Irish fairy door in Crosstown, I now have my own tiny fairy door about five inches tall on my desk next to my computer, and prepare to have visiting fairies at my home in Murdock—only the good fairies are welcome. These fairies might be closely associated to the brownies, known to be cheery and helpful household spirit of the fairy race from Scotland and England. As a young girl I was a member of the Brownies, a branch of Girl Scouts, traditionally wearing brown uniforms and beanies with a little fairy figure. The brownies are associated with barn work and sheepherding, but as times change, I wonder if they would help me with my writing. No passports are required, so it should be an easy process to send out invitations to the Good People, a common reference to fairies in Ireland.

In my yard in Murdock, is a hedge of buckthorn to the east side, likely planted by my grandparents or great-grandparents sometime in the last century or earlier. A hedge with a similar name is blackthorns. According to Irish folklore, the blackthorns provide protection for humans from the fairy people.

September 14, 2018
Crosstown Cottage, Crosstown, Killarney, County Kerry, Ireland and Murdock, Minnesota

Today I am daydreaming about walking the hill to the Ogham standing stone in the Crosstown Cottage, but am in reality now back home in Murdock. My mind was concentrating on this cottage and the people I know in Ireland.

The next day, I receive an email from Olive about a fire in the cottage the day before, September 14, 2018. The Horgan family was watching their cottage in flames that very same day in the evening their time, while firefighters climbed on the roof near the area of kitchen and back door in the dark of night. A fire truck parked in front of the cottage, the same location I watch horses pass the front gate, and was amazed by the beauty of the enchanted little cottage, with views of Mangerton Mountain. White smoke billowed from the roof, with a large gaping holes of light illuminating the cottage from the road. The stone walls of the cottage remained after the fire, with the remainder of the structure destroyed.

It is fortunate there were no injuries from the fire, but Crosstown Cottage was completely restored a second time by the Horgan family, renting out their cottage again in 2020, after the pandemic restrictions were removed.

I await my return to Crosstown Cottage, and visit with Olive and the entire Horgan family over a cup of tea with an apple tart from Daly's, and inquire out about any fairy sightings. Crosstown Cottage and the Horgan family are now connected to me for life.

Crosstown Cottage, A Witness of Time

Old cottage by the road stands, holding two centuries of stories and secrets. Trimmed in white and green, in the Kerry cottage way, long and narrow, folks and names of days forgotten, rested in their bed, took refuge from the wind, rain, and famine. Heating food with turf, warming cold hearts, stands the hearth in the center. Dirt floors, chamber pots under beds, and no running water for most of your life.

The Great Famine was witness to and recorded in the minds and souls of people you kept safe, now with no names to recall or say.

Ladies making daily soda bread, making the sign of the cross, saying a blessing, and poking the bread with a knife to let out the fairies before baking in the fireplace.

The old ash tree behind the cottage is a reminder of ancient Irish mythology connected to nature.

Decisions forced inhabitants to move to the new world, or found death and peace under this roof. Little Crosstown Cottage, speak of your past, reveal your secrets! The country of Ireland, a free state of Ireland was formed in your life, with war and peace etched in your limestone, you stand old and wise, a benchmark of time. Your fire of 2018 caused distress, rebuilt in modern glory. A global pandemic raged in 2020, and your walls still stand strong, offering safety.

Today you welcome travelers from around the world, with Mangerton Mountain keeping watch, surrounding you. As the light falls from the sky, birds chirp from nearby trees, Crosstown Cottage bringing comfort to sleeping inhabitants resting in their beds.

Chapter 13

Finding Dromkerry

May 25, 2018
11:30 am, Crosstown Cottage
Killarney, County Kerry, Ireland
County Kerry, Roman Catholic, Parish of Milltown
Baptism of Ellen Brennan

May 12, 1820
Droumkerry (Dromkerry)
Father, Michael Brennan
Mother, Margaret Daly

THIS MORNING I RECEIVED AN EMAIL FROM MICHAEL Lynch, archivist at the Kerry Library in Tralee with details I was seeking about Ellen.

The closest reference to Ellen Brennan baptism of proximity to that date is a daughter of Michael Brennan of Dromkerry. Coincidentally, given the marriage address that you mention for Ellen, this is a Milltown Catholic Church Parish. Unless you are 100 percent sure that Knockanarroor is correct, this is a possibility for Ellen's origin; not just for the coincidence, but also the fact her marrying a Foley, one of the most common surnames in Milltown, and Killorglin area.

This Michael Brennan was married firstly to Margaret Daly, but had four additional children between 1827 and 1834, namely Timothy, Michael, Mary and Margaret with the mother's name given as Johanna Daly.

Ellen Brennan, born 1820
Timothy Brennan, born 1827
Michael Brennan, born 1829
Mary Brennan, born 1832
Margaret Brennan, born 1834
The details were all new to me, opening the line of reasoning that

Ellen's mother Margaret Daly died at her birth or at least in the first four years of life. Johanna Daly is likely a sister, cousin or a relative of Ellen's mother. The baptism record is May 12, 1820, known birth date is May 15, 1820, are very close, and there is no other Ellen Brennan recorded for the Killarney area. The facts point toward Margaret Daly and Michael Brennan as Ellen's parents. Ellen likely did not know her mother or was too young to remember her. This tragic story has been a secret or was hidden for nearly two hundred years from my family, only uncovered in 2018.

These new details also point to Michael Brennan and Margaret Daly are my great-great-great-grandparents. Although I've found no marriage record for Michael and Margaret, it does not mean they were not married, rather not part of the available marriage records. The National Library of Ireland's surviving registers, digitally accessible online, indicate surviving baptism records beginning from October 1825, and marriages from October 1821 forward.

Lynch shared with me that Ellen Brennan baptism record seems to be very much "an outlier," as he can't find any other baptisms in Milltown Parish as early as 1820. He also indicates he agrees with my idea that it seems likely that Margaret died, and that Johanna was related to her – it was a fairly regular occurrence for a widower to take the next in line as a replacement wife! There is a marriage record for Michael to his second wife Johanna Daly of Droumkerry, March 2, 1824, at Milltown Parish in County Kerry.

⚜

It's 10 pm, the eve before going to Dromkerry, and I am excited to find the location of Ellen's origins in rural County Kerry. The owner and host of Crosstown Cottage, Olive Horgan, shared my excitement as I could barely sleep after an emotional conversation with Olive lasting until about 2:30 am, excited and tired at the same time. The conversation started with drinking Barry's Irish tea and asking Olive to wait as I rushed to the stone cottage bedroom to grab my notebook.

This old cottage was built in the traditional Kerry style, long and narrow with small windows, refurbished in recent years with modern conveniences. Staying May 11 to June 1, 2018, this lovely cottage gave me only a glimpse of what it was like to live in a dwelling not unlike what my Irish ancestors lived in, but of course without running water, electricity, modern toilets and plumbing, and the roof would have been thatched, unlike the current metal roof.

"Maybe Ellen was the only child of this woman Margaret Daily, she never knew her mother," said Olive. Sitting in front of the fireplace, we started to sketch all the possibilities in our minds, brainstorming as the new details emerged, knowing the hard facts will never be known. Johanna Daly, the woman Michael Brennan married in 1824, four years after Ellen's birth, could have been taking care of Ellen as a baby, and, we concur, was likely a sister, cousin, or relative of Margaret.

Olive looks for a fresh perspective, more personal, on the pain Ellen carried since birth, given the 1820 details of the baptism record associated with Dromkerry. "Ellen carried that hurt of her mother to Canada. Maybe you were meant to find out about her mother," said Olive.

I was having difficulty putting the pieces of my ancestors together to have a better understanding of their lives in Ireland, but to know exact details are lost, yet Olive thinks about the emotional or spiritual aspects I overlooked.

As we are talking, drinking more tea, we are now both crying. Olive is sitting in one of the two stuffed arm chairs, while I'm sitting on the sofa writing down each word of our conversation, thinking this would be a very meaningful evening, even if not shedding new light to my quest.

"Maybe your great-great-grandmother Ellen wanted you to speak her mother's name. Perhaps she did not get to know her own mother, or maybe call her by name," said Olive.

"I am crying," I said.

"So am I," said Olive.

"Even if you don't have all the relevant information, it is what fits together, it's what you know now. Ellen was born to Margaret Daly and Michael Brennan. You have the baptism record," Olive said.

Olive and I start to think about the time that has passed since the birth of Ellen, and the likely death of her mother Margret Daly. I start to calculate in my notebook 198 years as of 2018, almost two hundred years, and the month of Ellen's birth, May. Childbirth and death of a mother go hand in hand in earlier times and continue to be a risk in modern times. This was the month of Ellen's birth, appropriate we were having this talk.

"The words and name of Margaret Daly have not been spoken in 198 years. I think this is lovely," said Olive.

I share with Olive about the eight-foot-tall monument in Minnesota for Ellen, likely put up by her oldest son James. Again, Olive and I are crying, thinking about the lost and forgotten mother of Ellen.

Olive is the Irish friend I needed as I spliced my Irish roots together at her cottage I called home during my stay. She is yet another unexpected wonder I found in Ireland.

"You don't look American. If I had to pick you out of a room filled with people and say who is American, I would not select you with your red hair and features. I'd say you are Irish," said Olive.

After Olive departs Crosstown Cottage for her home next door at Stone Arch House, I think about my staying in the two-hundred-year-old cottage, dating back in style to the time of birth of Ellen. I am living in the cottage with a sense of home and belonging. It is not the building that makes a house a home, but the people like Olive and her family, or maybe a pig or other animals once kept in Irish cottages, as humans depended on animals for survival.

May 26, 2018
Townland Flintfield
County Kerry, Ireland

Olive, along with her son Kieran, age ten at the time of my visit, sets her GPS mapping in her car for directions to Dromkerry, complete with a posh Irish woman's accent, for a ten-mile drive, taking about twenty or more minutes total.

The directions to my ancestors' past from Crosstown to Dromkerry almost get us to our destination.

The GPS lets us know when we arrived in Dromkerry, but it was not actually apparent as there's no road sign, only fields, a few homes, sheep and no town. Along the roadside of R563, just north of the Ring of Kerry Road, Olive pulls over to the side of the road for me to take photos of a cottage in ruins, and sheep, grazing in the fields, an ewe and lambs. This would be the place I call Dromkerry, and the view that will remain in my mind, although it was not certain it was actually Dromkerry, except for the posh GPS Irish voice making the announcement of Dromkerry. Was I looking at the ruins of where Ellen and her family lived or maybe nearby? I will never know.

Standing on the side of the R563 Highway, located between the landmarks of the Golden Nugget Pub in Fossa to the east and Milltown to the west, I am thinking this is the closest I will come to the origins of my great-great-grandmother Ellen Brennan Foley in Townland Dromkerry. The former spelling is Droumkerry, now can be found on modern maps as Dromkerry.

The Irish meaning with Drom or Droum has been explained to me as hill or rear, meaning the hill or rear of Kerry, as in the county of Kerry in Ireland. Ireland was ice-covered during two glacial periods, leaving behind glacial deposits. A drumlin, or in Irish dromnín, meaning a small hill, are found all over the Irish landscape, thought to be created when glaciers were overloaded with sediment and left deposits as the power of the glaciers decreased.

In Ireland a townland is a geographic division of land, a grouping of farms and pastures, and extremely vital and helpful for tracing ancestors. The names to townlands in Ireland can describe the land, rooted in Irish descriptions, and a division of land system believed to date from Medieval times or before.

I commemorate the moment by picking up a piece of slate the size of my hand on the side of the road, near ruins of a cottage and grazing sheep.

In my field notebook I write: I have no way of knowing if this is the exact place my family lived. I will pack up the piece of slate and take it home.

It's common for rural roads in Ireland not to be marked, making it difficult to find roads, even with the help of GPS. It turns out I was not in Dromkerry, instead Townland Flintfield, missing the location by about one mile, west of the location of the roadside visit. I knew I needed more time to explore and find Dromkerry, even if it meant returning to Ireland for another visit.

I had almost found Dromkerry.

⚜

Continuing on the R563 from Dromkerry, Olive drives to Milltown, stopping at Kelly's Londis Petrol Station and Grocery, or what appeared to be the center of commerce, conveniently located next to Sacred Heart Catholic Church. Milltown's population is less than a thousand people, with pubs, schools, and businesses, including a Church of Ireland church.

Kelly's serves as a rest stop as I enjoy a vanilla ice cream cone with a flake, or stick of Cadbury chocolate inserted into the ice cream. Olive and Kieran had a Smooch, an ice cream shake with candy added, selecting toppings from a rotating trolley filled with candies and chocolates.

Milltown is significant as it is associated with Ellen's baptism, and the idea to find the associated church from 1820, or cemetery, likely linked to Ellen's family, including her mother Margaret Daly, whether factual, or the greatest possible outcome when there are so few details, and almost two hundred years has passed since Ellen's birth.

After departing Kelly's, we walk next door to the modern Sacred Heart Church, built in 1894, also the name of the church where I live in Murdock, Minnesota. Sacred Heart is a particular devotion and practice, especially to Irish Catholic, many with a framed image of Christ with his heart exposed, usually in a place of prominence in Irish homes, the same as I have. It originally belonged to my grandparents in Murdock.

Olive signed the Book of Prayer Intentions as we entered Sacred Heart in Milltown, and I put my signature to her words: "We are here to pray for Margaret Daly who gave birth to Ellen Brennan and who was baptized in Milltown in 1820. May she RIP wherever she is buried as we have no record. —Jannet Walsh, Murdock, Minnesota USA."

After lighting prayer candles, and praying for help, a woman cleaning and preparing the altar for Mass directed my party of three to Kilcolman Burial Ground and Killagh Priory, about one and a half miles outside of Milltown. From Sacred Heart Church, we watched for the sign for Killorglin on N70, turning to left, and followed to Abbeylands, L1223, a right turn. There was an impressive metal gate to open and a metal turnstile to walk through, followed by a short walk down a dirt road with green grass growing down the middle of the one-track road.

⚜

Now at Killagha Abbey, I walk in the footsteps of ancestors, as I must believe, and Saint Colman (530–606 AD) known to have built an earlier monastic foundation on the same site as Killagh Priory, according to historical information at the abbey. I see an Augustinian Abbey, now in ruins, built in 1216, and dedicated to Our Blessed Lady. During Killagh Priory's day it had lands and wealth, paying the third highest papal taxes in 1302. This was also part of the ancient Diocese of Ardfert in Ireland, an episcopal see or area of a bishop's authority, and the Prior was a Lord of Parliament, according to historic signs posted on the grounds. In 1649, Oliver Cromwell destroyed the building and cloister, and today only the priory ruins remain, with doors and niches made of red sandstone dating to the thirteenth century, and limestone work from the fifteenth century. Although the church has remained in ruins for more than three hundred years, the burial grounds are still in use today, including tombs and burial graves inside the walls of the church with no roof.

Walking down the dirt road is Patrick McKenna, a retired school teacher, author and historian from Milltown, accompanied by his border collie, colorings of black and white, a very common breed, especially for Irish farmers to herd sheep. McKenna is a graduate of University College Dublin, and was a secondary school teacher in Dublin, Tralee, and Africa, now retired and living in Milltown. After explaining my search for a grave of Margaret Daly, likely about 1820 to 1824, he was quick to join in my quest. McKenna mentions about 1820 or so many people only had a stone to mark their graves, no engraving, something reserved for the wealthy or gentry. He also says stones in an Irish cemetery should not be moved as they mark the site of a burial; that was something I could not imagine as I purchased engraved burial markers for my family, very detailed to avoid confusion in years to come.

"It's all higgledy-piggledy," said McKenna about the disorder of the burial sites. "I have the utmost respect of people searching. We are the lucky ones that stayed in Ireland. The people that left Ireland must have been homesick for a long time."

McKenna shared with me in the 1900s, his father's brothers, his uncles, six of eleven departed Ireland. None returned home. Unlike my family, there is a large memorial stone about shoulder's height erected near the entrance to the burial grounds for his family.

Joining in the conversation is Olive, "Hurt follows from one generation to the next generation. Go to the water where all our battles start. It is a healing process to stand in healing water." Olive on this day served as my guide to the past, including spiritual wisdom, while McKenna provided the history of Kilcolman Burial Ground and Killagha Abbey.

Facts now point to Margaret Daly being the mother of Ellen Brennan Foley. These burial grounds in Milltown, precisely where I stand in Kilcolman Burial Grounds, are where Saint Colman built a priory during his lifetime. The reality of possibilities is now in the center of my genealogy search, with solid facts not always possible. This, then, is perhaps the closest I will know to being accurate. Somewhere here Margaret Daly is buried with stones marking her grave.

"When one of my uncles died, they brought the coffin through the front of the abbey and out the side door and back to the front of the abbey. It was to say hello, and let all his neighbors know he had arrived," said McKenna. The neighbors are the dead buried at the abbey.

The glacial carved mountain range Slieve Mish on the eastern edge of Dingle Peninsula is the scenic setting of Killagha Abbey. McKenna mentioned the duties of the newly dead at Killagha Abbey near the banks of the River Maine. "At this graveyard people believed at the time of the burial, the first weeks were spent drawing the water to make the tea."

I wonder as someone is about to die, or to help ease the worries of the soon to be departed, if people talked in such a way, "You will soon be preparing tea at Killagha." It certainly is better than saying you are dying, giving a since of hope after death.

As I was walking around the abbey grounds, about ready to leave, I again felt disappointed with not finding a marker listing my relatives, especially Margaret Daly. Putting together many loose ends to tell my story of Irish heritage is more investigatory than I could have imagined.

While I take my final steps at Killagha, Olive asks me what I think about finding the graveyard of my ancestors. I am speechless. It's hard to process. I wish I could talk to my ancestors and ask them about their lives. I think I have pieced together the best possible story as is possible.

Olive replied, "You are going to put an end to the story. There will be closure of the story of Ellen Brennan. I think you are lucky to get so much information from before the Famine and go back as far as 1820. More than likely Margaret Daly is buried here in at Killagha Abbey, with no marker."

June 1, 2018
En Route from Crosstown Cottage to Killarney Railway Station
Killarney, County Kerry, Ireland

It's time to return home to America and leave my friends the John and Olive Horgan family, living east of Killarney town, and Crosstown Cottage.

Knowing I was in the last minutes of departure from Crosstown Cottage before taking a morning train to Dublin from the Killarney railway station, I document the cottage by taking last-minute photos and videos of the interior, and pose with members of the Horgan family outside of the cottage. Its trim is white and green, its walls of natural lime and field stone, appear to be once covered in whitewash with traces of white along the edges of the stones.

Olive offered to take me to the Killarney train station, and I gladly accepted the offer as a final opportunity to spend time with her. I sat next to her in the left side seat as she drove in her right-side drive car. I mentioned my desire to return at to Ireland, maybe at Christmas in 2018, as I was determined to discover more about Dromkerry, and find a more exact location of my family origins in Ireland.

Olive was driving her car wearing a light blue blouse and fashionable Jackie O-styled sunglasses, her son Kieran, age ten, wears his school uniform complete with tie, school emblem on his sweater; and Darren, age twenty-two, a white and blue navy striped tee shirt, just home from college, we pass McDonald's restaurant on Park Road, about two miles from the train station.

I can't remember if I started singing or Olive, but an impromptu choir of "Christmas in Killarney" song broke out en route to the train station, slightly different wording in the opening line with holly tree, instead of holly green.

"OK, let's start it again," said Olive, directing with her left-hand pointer finger as a choir conductor, and right hand on the wheel.

"The holly tree, the ivy tree. The prettiest picture you ever seen. It's Christmas in Killarney with all the folks at home."

At the station, my luggage unloaded from the car, I stand alone as Olive blows kisses in the air fanning them with her hands toward me, with yet another song.

"So long, farewell, auf wiedersehen, goodbye. Goodbye to you, and you and you and you. Jannet be safe! Text me tonight from Dublin."

With two quick honks on Olive's car horn, she drives away from the train station. I was about to depart the same Killarney train station my father visited in 1953 heading to Dublin, the capitol city of Ireland. As the train started to slowly back out of the station, I started to cry as I am leaving behind my Irish friends, and land where my family has roots. If I could return at Christmas, I would make plans and do my best to make it happen.

Christmas Day 2018
Our Lady of the Valley
Beaufort Townland, Black Valley,
County Kerry, Ireland

It was in July 2018 that I made the decision to return to Ireland at Christmas and continue my quest to unearth my family's past and connections to Dromkerry Townland. Unable to stay at Crosstown Cottage because of a fire, I made plans to find another cottage to serve as my Irish research headquarters.

I'm driving my rental car from Shamrock Cottage in the Gap of Dunloe in the Black Valley, nestled between the MacGillycuddy's Reeks mountain range to the west and the Purple Mountain Group, to Mass at Our Lady of the Valley Catholic Church, over a half mile away. I contemplated walking, but was not sure if it would be raining or not on Christmas Day.

Shamrock Cottage is fifteen miles from Dromkerry, and I planned to try to connect with people at the church, maybe make connections to help me set foot where Ellen lived. I am part journalist and part worshiper, praying for help to connect the missing pieces in my genealogy research.

After arriving at Our Lady of the Valley, built in 1955, I have no problem parking, and find premium parking outside the front entrance. I did a U-turn and parked on the left side of the road—that's the correct side in Ireland—and pointed back toward the Shamrock Cottage. I didn't want to make special maneuvers in front of the parish members to show them my American driving skills or lack thereof. Almost moments after stepping out of the car, I was greeted by a gentleman from the parish who introduced me to a parish priest from Killarney.

My introduction to the priest was met with Irish humor, as the same man who greeted me, told me I was in the presence of the Bishop of Black Valley. There was no evidence of a bishop's crosier, miter or ecclesiastical ring to kiss, so I said I was honored to meet him in case he was a bishop appearing at Mass.

The Reverend Father, although not a bishop, inquired about my visit. I explained I needed help connecting with people in Dromkerry and was searching for the origin of my family, and would appreciate any help. I was assured at or by the end of Mass that I would have connections.

I fit in here like I was back home in my church in Murdock. Before the Concluding Rites, Father asks the women to sing a verse of "Silent Night" followed by the men, and then women and men altogether. It was very lovely, listening to the old and young voices blend together in the Black Valley. The start to finish of Christmas Mass ended in approximately thirty-five minutes, a possible land speed record.

I thanked the priest mentioned as local bishop of the valley as I existed the church and gathered outside in the front lawn as parishioners reconvened outside to visit. I could not help but think I belonged to Our Lady of Black Valley or at least the people I had connected to, in some small way. The original gentleman I met at the church came through for me with a list of families in Dromkerry, suggesting I connect with them. I was prepared to visit Dromkerry tomorrow. I would visit Dromkerry on St. Stephen's Day, the Irish version of Boxing Day, generally celebrated simply visiting with family. It seems appropriate for a day I plan to connect with family history nearly two centuries ago. I await for what my quest will reveal in Dromkerry.

St. Stephen's Day
December 26, 2018
Townland Dromkerry,
County Kerry, Ireland

As I travel down a narrow road marked as Kerry Woollen Mills between the Ring of Kerry Road, N72, and road to Milltown, R563, I monitor my Global Positioning System on my iPhone and rental car to see if I've arrived in Dromkerry. I notice two walkers on the side of the road near a grove of trees out for an afternoon stroll on St. Stephen's Day. I use the opportunity to connect to Dromkerry.

"I'm looking for Dromkerry," I shout out the front passenger window, right side in Ireland.

The young sporty looking woman replies, "You are here. This is Dromkerry!"

I introduce myself first while the car motor is running, explain about my quest to find Dromkerry and my connection with my family.

I am directed down the road to get to a farm in Dromkerry. I can't thank them enough for helping the strange American trying to piece together her Irish family history.

After the Dromkerry couple helped me sketch a quick map of the area, we waved goodbye and I was traveling again on the unnamed road in the Townland of Dromkerry. As I reached the main road to Milltown, I drove a short distance to the west, then turned on to a small road that would take me to the farm on which my family might have lived and worked before or around 1820. I was also ascending in elevation as I traveled up the unpaved narrow road. The Ordnance Survey map of Ireland, map 78, lists the elevation at the highest point in Dromkerry at 106 meters, or more than 347 feet.

After receiving a local farmer's permission, I passed through the open farm gate, and parked near the old stone barn and house dating to about two hundred years old, I would learn.

The view from Dromkerry looking south could not be more beautiful as I was looking directly at the Gap of Dunloe, the MacGillycuddy's Reeks mountain range to the west and the Purple Mountain Group to the east. At this perspective, I'm about ten to fifteen miles away Shamrock Cottage. I can see the Lakes of Killarney from this vantage point. I am standing here looking at some of the most beautiful landscape in all of Ireland. Is this what my family left behind? Why was the story of the beauty of the landscape not passed down to me?

The wind is blowing hard, it's sunny and cloudy at the same time as I walk near the cow shed trying to understand the mountainous landscape and ancient Irish farm dwellings as a visitor. There are huge black clouds floating over the Gap of Dunloe in the distance. The sun is peeking behind the clouds. This is certainly a breathtaking view, but to understand the struggles of life and survival from the 1800s, I'm not sure what my family thought of this view.

Ellen's family could not have dreamed of modern bathroom conveniences and water flowing from a tap in the cottage they lived in at Dromkerry. I struggle to understand the fuel stove at Shamrock Cottage to keep warm, burning holly wood and turf, and take out the ashes in the morning.

Ellen's family were tenants of the Herbert Family, English and protestant landlords, connected to the Muckross House of Killarney, according to census records. They did not own the cottage they lived in or the land they worked, as was common for poor Irish Catholics in the 1800s. The Irish people were ruled by the British in their own island of Ireland.

This proud Irish farm has about three hundred Friesian cattle. The farm once had little cottages around the land. If you stand at the highest point of Dromkerry, the view includes the Gap of Dunloe, the Lakes of Killarney, Killorglin, and Tralee.

❧

I can imagine Ellen and her family walking between the ash and apple trees near the cow shed, looking over the mountainous scenery from Dromkerry and thinking they were on the top of the world, as the clouds seem to be closer to earth from the hill. Certainly, heaven can be directly overhead in Dromkerry. The view is heavenly, breathtaking and will be recorded in my mind for years to come.

It is possible Ellen's mother, Margaret Daly, died giving birth to her, or sometime afterward here in Dromkerry, not far from where I stand hypnotized by the Irish countryside. No matter if I am standing at the correct farm or townland, I am very close to where my family lived and worked. It is possible I am walking in the Brennan family footsteps. I think my Irish family would be pleased I am here to see their origins in Townland Dromkerry.

St. Stephen's Day
December 26, 2018
Kate Kearney's Cottage
Gap of Dunloe
County Kerry, Ireland

I check my email while waiting for my meal of pan-fried salmon with mashed potatoes and carrots to be served at Kate Kearney's Cottage nestled at the entrance to the Gap of Dunloe, separating the MacGillycuddy's Reeks mountain range from the Purple Mountain Group. Kate's has been serving travelers since before the Great Famine, and is famous for once serving an illicit strong drink poitín or poteen, pronounced potcheen, also referred to as Kate Kearney's Mountain Dew, according to the family-run establishment's history. I ordered coffee, and no poitín. I make conversation with a young woman seated next to me from the state of Virginia surrounded by her Irish and American family, sharing our travel stories.

There are fiddles, accordions, and the voices of young Irish men part of The Rising, a traditional Irish music group, preforming as I read one of the most significant emails in my iPhone I have received about my family research on this trip or perhaps about my family history quest altogether.

The late Jeremiah "Jerry" Fitzgerald of Dromkerry had knowledge about the Brennan family living in a little house which was a fallen down little cottage and trees overgrown in a haggard. Today there are no remains, but only now green grassland, pasture for the cows and farm animals. This location of Brennan cottage is about three fields north down the farm road after walking to a high point or peak, and descending to a field occupied by a bull on the day I visited.

I am extremely thankful for the personal knowledge of Jerry, likely among the few, if not only remaining people with direct information of a cottage that is now lost in time. My timing is also on spot, as this information would otherwise be simply lost for all times.

Jerry gave me an incredible gift of knowledge I can share with future generations of my family's origin story in Dromkerry, County Kerry, Ireland. History and memories are very fragile, ready to disappear into the landscape, just as the stone cottage my family once called home. Blessed is the memory of Jerry, and all the people, past and present, that once called Dromkerry home.

I will return to Dromkerry before the end of my trip and walk close as possible to my family's origins in Ireland. St. Stephen's Day in Ireland is about family. I have now put pieces of my family back together again.

December 30, 2018
Townland Dromkerry
County Kerry, Ireland

I prepare my expeditionary team to ascend the hill of my ancestors, walk as close as possible to where the location of Ellen's family lived dating to at least 1820, a spot known as the Brennan cottage.

The Horgan family of Crosstown agreed to join me on my Dromkerry adventure. Olive and husband John, and their sons Kieran and Johnaton gathered, and we drove to Dromkerry in two cars. I drive with Olive as a passenger, and John in the other car, serving as the front vehicle, armed with maps I provided to mark our destination. We were time traveling almost two centuries back in my family's Irish history. At the Catholic church in Fossa, our expedition's basecamp, we consolidated to one car, making it easier to travel on the narrow roads ahead at Dromkerry, with a total now of five passengers.

After making necessary turns and maneuvers, we reached the unmarked road on Dromkerry, a dirt road. John drove, while I gave directions from memory, and Johnaton continued to follow the map and GPS from the passenger's front seat, left side.

The large metal farm gate was closed, so I jumped out of the car, along with Johnaton, to open the lock and hold the gate open for the car to pass through. After the car was parked by the old stone barn, the first obstacle was a live wire electrical fence. I don't remember all the details, but John helped lift the wire as we all passed under it in a form of farmyard limbo, and no injuries.

We walk north up the hill to a peak, and of course there is a need to watch each step as we were at a farm, and cattle have left scatological reminders along the path. After reaching the peak of the hill, we look back to the south at the cow shed, old cottage and barn, a piggery, with a view or the Gap of Dunloe, Lakes of Killarney and the mountains of Killarney. We continue walking north and descend the hill and start to walk the length of three fenced pasture fields from the peak. There is a yet another gate to open, with a blue rope for double insurance to keep it closed.

I open the two large sliding bolts and swing the gate open, and my walking stops. As there is a bull grazing in the field, I make a decision we have come far enough, and it was time for the photo session to start. Olive waits on the other side of the gate as she is not wanting to be near the bull, and John takes photos. The sky is cloudy and overcast, but not raining, and the pastures are rich colors of green. It is a short distance to the field of my family's origins, but a bull is now living where I need to go. I now stand as close as possible to the origins of Ellen and her family. I consider each step I walk to be sacred here at Dromkerry.

Olive takes photos of me after I finish the photo session with John, returning to the other side of the farm gate. As I walk back up the hill with the Horgan family, there is a discussion about my ancestors. Could this be the home Ellen departed from Ireland to North America? I will never know. The beautiful green pasture could be the very place where a cow or sheep were raised and sold to help pay for her Ellen's passage to Canada. The milk produced in County Kerry is famous for high fat content in butter, and could have also been a source of income to support emigration. Ellen's dowry for marriage, and a new life was likely supported by the very fields I walk past today.

Seeing the grazing lands of Dromkerry, it is a scene nearly scripted by a movie scout, wanting to find rolling landscape to set a movie in Ireland. As we reach the peak of the hill, I stop and take photos of the Horgan family with the landscape of Killarney and a cow shed in the background. My red hair set off by the green of an insulated trench coat, and high waterproof leather boots will be how I look on a December 30, 2018, visit to Dromkerry.

❧

I swing open the main gate to the farm as John drives through. This time I close the gate by myself, making sure the two sliding locks are secure. As I get in the car to join the Horgan family, John says, "Jannet, you look like you belong here."

I must have closed the gate with great ease to receive such a compliment. The truth is, I was delighted to connect with the landscape of my family's most likely origins, didn't let any cows go missing, and the bull has claimed the area my ancestors lived, worked and breathed the Irish air.

The sacrifice of Ellen and all Irish emigrants leaving Ireland behind, is a selfless act of love. The pain of a broken heart for family and a homeland can't be repaired. I think the understanding for me rests in the fact I am the recipient, along with my family, of a life in America. If Ellen would have stayed in Ireland and experienced the Great Famine, her chances of success and survival would be limited, and possibility a sentence of death. Ellen's emigration gives life for generations to come.

Dromkerry has taken a bit of my heart. In my quest to learn more about my Irish family, this appears to be a successful mission. I await to see what might come in future expeditions.

Today I complete my great-great-grandmother Ellen's journey home from North America to Ireland, almost two hundred years since she departed Dromkerry. This is an unexpected pleasure and honor of my life.

ᘯᒪ

Dromkerry Townland

Dromkerry connects the past to present.
Dromkerry gives life to the cattle in its green pastures.
Dromkerry feeds the hungry beyond its stone field walls.
Dromkerry is where life starts, ends and begins again.
Dromkerry gives meaning to being an Irish emigrant.
Dromkerry is land of Ireland's sons and daughters.
Certainly, heaven can be directly overhead in Dromkerry.

Chapter 14

Exile from Ireland: Irish Port of Cobh

December 27, 2018
Cobh Town, County Cork, Ireland
WatersEdge Hotel, Westbourne Place

I JUST ARRIVED IN THE CITY OF COBH, PRONOUNCED cove or "cove-ff," an island situated in the Cork Harbour, on the south coast of County Cork, Ireland. The port city has gone by other names, including Queenstown, 1849 to 1920, changed after a visit by Queen Victoria when England ruled the entire island of Ireland; now United Kingdom rules only Northern Ireland.

Driving almost two hours and more than eighty miles while getting lost several times even using maps and GPS navigation, I started just after a late sunrise, about 9 am, at Shamrock Cottage, high in the Gap of Dunloe in County Kerry. Exhaustion overtakes me from my travels driving on the right side of my rental car, an automatic transmission Volkswagen Passat. If you saw a car driving slowly on N22 Highway east toward Cobh this morning, it was likely me when you honked. I now know slow traffic should keep left on the freeways in Ireland, not the right side of the road. By now I should be accustomed to driving in Ireland, with practical left-hand side of road driving experience from previous trips. My American mind thinks I'm driving on the wrong side of the road, but the license plates are clearly marked, IRL 181-D-35775, in Irish, Baile Átha Cliath, Éire, or Dublin, Ireland. I'm in Ireland!

The Passat is now safely parked next to the Cork Harbour, tucked under the WatersEdge Hotel's lower deck on Westbourne Place, requiring precision driving down the hill to the harbor. For two nights I am calling the hotel "home" from room 17. The view from my room is spectacular, looking at the Cork Harbour. It may be not unlike that which my great-great-grandmother Ellen Brennan Foley last viewed Ireland between 1836 and 1841, before boarding a ship with a final destination of British North America, the former territories belonging to the British Empire, now known as Canada. I will never be certain if Cobh is the exact place of departure for Ellen before reaching New Brunswick, Canada, as no immigration records have been found. Yet it was known ships departed Canada with timber, returning with passengers as ballast, giving returning ships human cargo for stability. New Brunswick's primary export was timber, and ships were modified to carry passengers in the holds, or below deck, lowering fares, allowing more Irish to emigrate, averaging a six-week journey. The phrase timber in, passengers out was a slogan of this period, timber in the ships from Canada, passengers out from Ireland. Travelers battled difficult shipboard conditions of poor sanitation, diseases such as typhus and more, lack of ventilation, insufficient food, and were lucky if they even made it to Canada, as many ships were lost as sea.

Cobh has a natural harbor with a maritime and emigration legacy, the last port of call for the RMS Titanic in 1912, and rescue station for survivors of the RMS Lusitania sunk by a German U-Boat in 1915, according to local history. I have come to walk the streets of Cobh and take in the views of the harbor flowing to the Celtic Sea and finally to the North Atlantic Ocean. I want to see the last views of Ireland, taken in and recorded in the mind of thousands upon thousands of Irish immigrants heading to North American and Australia, voluntary or involuntary.

Seated next to the hotel window I am overlooking Haulbowline Island, the naval headquarters for the Irish Naval Service. I know it is the naval island, as a young waitress so informed me while delivering an open face salmon sandwich to the table. Currently little traffic moves in the harbor except for a large Irish Navy vessel and small boats; perhaps one is a tugboat, navigating the waters on the left, or port side if I were in a ship, and not at my table for lunch.

Located next to my hotel are cruise ships docked, Cobh Heritage Centre, along with the Irish Railway Station, or in Irish, Iarnród Éireann. I'll search for information about my family and Irish immigration, but have little hope of finding new details. If that did happen—even the tiniest pebble to add to my genealogy search of my Irish American heritage—would be a welcome surprise.

Looking out to the Cork Harbour, a small vessel or perhaps a raft, passes by my lookout and table, but I am unsure if the vessel is Irish Navy or a leisure craft. Next is a yellow and black pilot boat, marked Cork Pilot, responsible for piloting larger vessels in the harbor. If this is the harbor from which Ellen departed Ireland, how did she get from

Killarney, nearly eighty miles away? Where did she stay in Cobh? I'm hoping to piece together what is possible in the next few days—like an Irish family history detective. In this case, it is the exile of Ellen from the island of Ireland I'm here to discover. It is possible departing Ireland was her only way to survive, yet staying in Ireland, as history tells, likely was sure starvation or death as the result of the Great Famine. I would not be in Cobh today trying to put pieces together if Ellen had stayed; this is speculation, but the real fact is one million died from starvation and related diseases during the famine. Even though Ellen left Ireland before the famine, there were still shortages of food in Ireland.

December 27, 2018
St. Colman's Cathedral, Cobh Town

I start my ascent up the hill to St. Colman's Cathedral from the Titanic Memorial at Pearse Square, and looking back at the harbor, can see the White Star Line Office. Turning right on to Rahilly Street, the ascent becomes steeper by almost every step on the narrow road lined with homes. Switching back to the left at Cathedral Place, I walk uphill as the road curves to the right at the Cathedral's front entrance. Here I stop to look back over the harbor yet again. Looking out to the harbor, I look directly down on the rooftops of homes, white smoke billowing from chimney stacks, the smell of peat distinct. From the aerial view I'm seeing the backside of residential homes on West View, a slated uphill street with a group of colorful homes called the Deck of Cards. These houses were built on a hill, and if one would fall, so goes the saying, all the houses would fall like a deck of cards. Sea gulls fly over the row of houses as I continue to turn toward the west, now facing the front of the Cathedral.

The carillon bells sounded at fifteen minutes before 3 pm, as I find a pew near the main altar, wanting to rest and pray at St. Colman's Cathedral. Construction started for the cathedral in 1868, with the first Mass celebrated in 1879, and consecrated and dedicated to St. Colman in 1919. The forty-nine-bell carillon is one of the largest in Ireland. Ireland's largest bell is called St. Colman, weighing almost four tons. The port of Cobh serves as a natural amphitheater to the cathedral bells; since becoming part of the landscape it has sent hail and farewell to visitors and countless Irish emigrants. The cathedral was built on the site of the existing parish church of St. John the Baptist, built in 1810. A prison was located next to the church.

If Cobh is the location from which Ellen departed, then it was St. John the Baptist Church where she likely prayed before setting sail for North America.

Sitting in the pew, I remove my sweater, light jacket and winter overcoat in an attempt to cool down from the difficult and steep walk from the harbor uphill to the Cathedral. Another fifteen minutes passes, the carillon bells sound, marked with three bells ringing at 3 pm. At the same time, ships blow horns in Cork Harbour. Young families with children are gathering around the nativity scene to the right of the altar and a Christmas tree with lights is left of the altar.

Now 3:15 pm, I can't stop noticing the line and people packing a pew a row behind me, clicking their cameras shutters and, more quietly, their phones. Hanging from the ceiling is a large red perpetual lamp or altar lamp as a reminder of Christ's presence. Just as I sit and pray, I continue to think of Ellen before departing Ireland.

I can imagine Ellen lighting a candle as the visitors do today for special intentions and prayers for safe travel, as well as for family members left behind in Ireland, the motherland. These prayers no doubt included tears falling on her hands, rosary and clothing. The pain would be so difficult to bear; Ellen's body was likely weak from crying, the same as mourning a death at a funeral. For it was mourning of leaving behind everything familiar. Now there is a humming of voices about the cathedral, as there was during Ellen's time, yet I think then likely people would have been crying and wailing, something Irish called keening, public crying in grief at a wake or funeral. She was a young woman, between sixteen and twenty-one or so, when she left her world behind in Ireland. She may as well have been about to launch into outer space, so foreign would the trip have been.

I want to envision Ellen as she was on the day she boarded a ship to Canada, or at least started her journey, stopping at other ports before arriving in North America. She was likely wearing her best and only clothing, carrying some small piece of luggage, maybe not even that. I can imagine her having a rosary, a good handkerchief and something small to reminder of home near Killarney. Did she carry a small stone, or even a handful of soil, wrapped in one of her handkerchiefs? For me, I would need something that is of the land, a reminder of the place I called home, as only memories can be carried safety in Ellen's mind, causing both pain and joy.

At 3:30 pm, the bells are again ringing. Now I think about Ellen and her walk down to the harbor from the cathedral. Could it be I am walking where she once walked? Again, I will never know as I lack the facts about her departure and arrival to Canada. The walk ascending to the cathedral was one of the most difficult walks I can ever remember walking in a town in Ireland, or any municipality. The descent could be extremely dangerous if streets are slippery or icy, let alone combined with being filled with fear and grief stricken of soon-to-be Irish emigrants. If only the bricks and covered pavement could reveal the stories of the people walking the streets during the time of Ellen, I would know more. I could add one more pebble to my collection of knowledge.

It is now 4 pm, and, dipping my fingers in the holy water, I depart the cathedral and make the Catholic sign of the cross. This I have no doubt Ellen did this countless times. The Irish are known for making the sign of the cross simply when passing a church, not a custom I know as a child. The sun is starting to set as the winter days are short in Ireland.

Walking down from the cathedral to the harbor, I stand to watch as a sailor climbs into small dinghy at the Lusitania Pier. My mind drifts to the diminishing horizon line, the sky darkening into night.

December 27, 2018
WatersEdge Hotel, Cobh Town

Looking out to the Cork Harbour from my window in room 17, WatersEdge, I start to think about my need to connect to a place and landscape of my Irish ancestors. What could be the origin of this desire? It could be my ancestors are part of the landscape, buried in sacred and not-so-sacred locations, forgotten in unmarked graves with only stones to mark a life once lived and loved.

When specific places can be identified, like a townland, cottage, farm, I can walk in the footprints of family forgotten. I crave to give understanding, bring a sense of identity and belonging for myself, possibility for those who may one day call me their ancestor. I want a story to call my own about my Irish family, perhaps the story my father and the rest of his family did not have.

The many qualities of being Irish didn't start to disappear the moment Ellen or other emigrants stepped on the ships in Cobh; that could be attributed to centuries of influence of the English rule, Normans, Vikings, and other invaders. Henry VIII and the Penal Laws imposed on the Irish people, both Catholic and Protestants, to force acceptance of the Anglican Church. Bishops associated with the cathedral in Cobh died in exile during the Penal years, approximately 1691 to 1769, according to St. Colman's Cathedral history.

There is no way of knowing if Ellen or other family members were still speaking Irish when they departed Ireland on the cusp of the Great Famine. Irish was the language of most people in Ireland up to the late 1700s. The Irish language was associated with poverty, along with a lack of speaking English at the beginning of the 1800s.

Of the eight million or so people in Ireland 1841, an estimated two-and-a-half million were Irish speakers, or about 30 percent. The Great Famine, 1845–1849, resulted in the death of about one million people, and the emigration of approximately one-and-a-half million. The Famine took a deadly total on the population of Irish speaker, with death or emigration adding to rapid decline of the Irish language, later resulting in movement called the Gaelic Revival of Irish culture.

It is possible Ellen attended a school in rural County Kerry called a Hedge School, a secret school for Catholics or other non-conforming, such as Presbyterians, in Ireland. The British ruled the Irish people in Ireland, promoting their Anglican Church and English language. The Hedge Schools were often in outside random locations teaching basics, but also included Greek and Latin. These illegal schools were a form of resistance to British colonization and a way to preserve Irish language and culture.

National schools in Ireland were established after 1831 to promote the English language, not Irish for the Irish people in their own land. If so, Ellen was learning English in the strict curriculum of de-Irishing education, with students wearing a wooden tally stick hung around necks.

Robert Wilson Lynd, 1879–1949, an Irish writer and essayist, states the tally sticks were to be marked by a notch at home by parents each time the child spoke Irish. This means Irish children were being taught by their Irish parents not to be Irish. Survival meant being English: speaking English and survival in Ireland were synonymous for the Irish. This all helps explain why I heard no Irish language spoken at home in Murdock. This is another reason for Ellen to depart Ireland. The story of oppression by an outside ruling class is all too familiar in history, with hints of what the US government did to the American Indian school children, teaching them something they were not—teaching them to be English-speaking Americans.

Homesickness is nonproductive and could even be deadly. Imagine Irish immigrants needing to forget Ireland in order to survive their passage and make new homes abroad. Few details passed from my Irish ancestors from Ireland; no Irish songs passed from my father to me. Assimilation likely meant survival, learned originally in

Ireland, and continued in North America. In the case of Ellen's oldest son, James G. Foley, born in Maine, he assimilated by serving in the American Civil War.

✌

The lights from Haulbowline Island are shining into room number 17 from across the Cork Harbour, but it is pitch dark and foggy— too difficult to see the docked Irish Naval ships. The naval base on Haulbowline, known to be the home of the first yacht club in the world, 1720, is connected by a bridge to the island of Cobh, all connected to the island of Ireland.

✌

Finishing my breakfast in the hotel restaurant, I think about the day and what I might find or not find out about Cobh as a possible point of departure from Ireland for my family. I keep calm, yet would be grateful for any suggestions that might be learned about Ellen departing Ireland.

My appointment started at 11 am with Christy Keating, a tall gentleman and genealogist at the Cobh Heritage Centre located almost next door to the WatersEdge Hotel. I arrived about fifteen minutes early. After some quick searching, it became evident I would not find details if my Ellen departed from Cobh, between 1836 and 1841, however numerous resources encouraged me to continue my search.

Christy suggested Cobh was the most likely port for Ellen to depart as it was the closest from Killarney. Tralee likely was a second choice, and Limerick as third. In the midst of a great deal of uncertainty, it was very helpful to have a genealogist provide possibilities when the actual location Ellen last walked in Ireland and viewed from the Cobh Harbour are lost in time.

Getting help from Christy is like working with your favorite uncle or father, except he has resources at his fingertips, and knowledge all rolled together in one Irish body. He thinks a likely way Ellen got to Cobh from Killarney is by pony and cart on the Butter Roads, the highway of the 1800s and before. Irish farmers' butter was transported on the ancient roads to the Butter Market in Cork, sold and exported around the world. Butter produced from cows in the lush green pastures in County Kerry and other locations in Ireland was excellent for exporting. Its fat content was high, meaning it could last longer aboard ships. "All roads led to the butter market," said Christy. "Ellen could have stayed in sheds along the way to Cobh, getting food along the way."

I had my own thoughts about what Ellen might have carried, but wanted to hear Christy's thoughts. "She carried nothing, maybe a small bag she made from pigskins, or a cloth. She wore a jacket, hat and coat, with bits in her bag of food, items small from home. It's likely her bag was made from a flour sack. I feel your entire family left, not just Ellen. Her parents could have arranged a dowry, sold cows or sheep. Sell a cow and there is your dowry to get married in Canada," said Christy.

I wanted to know Christy's thoughts for reasons of Ellen's departure from Ireland before the Great Famine. When the Penal Laws were repealed, about 1829, Irish Catholics were free to travel outside of Ireland. There was less demand of Irish crops and supplies after the end of the Napoleonic War supporting the English Army, along with crop failure and food shortages, all contributing to Ellen leaving Ireland, according to Christy.

Christy located details of a Michael Brennan, of Killorglin was found in 1853 living in a house located on Lonart (possibly Langford St.), the main street in Killorglin, according to the 1840 census. This town is located on the famous Ring of Kerry road, and known for the famous Puck Fair goat festival each year. One legend is that a male goat, a puck, is believed to have saved the town in ancient times against an invasion of Oliver Cromwell. It is possible the Michael Brennan living in Killorglin was Ellen's father or a family member, but that is unknown, just as the legend of the goat saving the town. Legend or fact?

My visit with the genealogist lasted more than an hour, leaving me exhausted and hungry for lunch. Creamed vegetable soup, bread and butter from Cork, followed by a Café Americano coffee at the little restaurant at Cobh Heritage Center helped restore my strength and spirits. Although I didn't receive any definite information about Ellen's departure, I did gain more information potentially surrounding her departure from Ireland. Knowing Cobh is a very likely place of departure for Ellen from Ireland, I walked the streets, visited the Cathedral, like so many who depart Ireland from Cobh, never to return.

Walking along the waterfront on West Beach Street to see more of the town of Cobh, I encounter the Rob Roy, a bar located at Pearse Square, with engraved marble sign about the RMS Titanic and the former Rob Roy Hotel. In the 1880s and early 1900s, Irish emigrant farewell gatherings were known as American Wakes. These wakes were similar to a traditional Irish funeral wakes to celebrate the loss of a family member, but instead were for people still alive and emigrating from Ireland to America, saying enough last goodbyes to last a lifetime.

Wanting to learn more, I entered the Rob Roy, and enjoyed a cup of hot tea, talking with the barman, and guests. It was at this very location countless American Wakes had taken place in the former hotel. Cobh was the last port of call for the Titanic in 1912 before striking an iceberg and sinking. The ship was anchored in the harbor all within view of the White Star Line Building where I enjoy my tea. I imagine Ellen had an American Wake back home in Dromkerry surrounded by family, and perhaps here in Cobh, not far from the Rob Roy, filled with sadness.

December 28, 2018
Waters Edge Hotel, Cobh Town
11:50 pm

I hear motoring, sounds of a large ship, and jump out of bed and look out the hotel window. The humming noise almost makes my bed vibrate from the huge ferry passing in the harbor. The ferry service from Brittany Ferries was likely arriving from Roscoff, France. The noise and vibrations of the ferry are probably common to residents in Cobh, similar to the trains at home in Murdock, shaking homes and engine whistling in approaching the railroad crossing.

In the morning I will drive back to Shamrock Cottage in the Gap of Dunloe, my home in Ireland during this visit to Killarney.

This trip to Ireland puts together more pieces from my family's Irish past, and while I can't put them all back together again, it is more than I had before my visit to Cobh.

If in the future, when I'm asked from where my family departed from in Ireland, I can now say with confidence, most likely Cobh Harbour. I can tell of the sloped streets, rainy days, ship horns, ferries shaking my bed, bells ringing to mark the hours at St. Colman's Cathedral, and my view of the port from room 17 at the WatersEdge Hotel in Cobh town.

Chapter 15

Ϭales of Ϭwo Dublins: Dublin Farm,

Dublin Fair City

October 6, 2018
Dublin Farm, Murdock, Minnesota
Dublin Township, Swift County, Minnesota

I STAND ON THIS SACRED LAND AT DUBLIN FARM WITH the remains of corn husks and stalks harvested a few days ago by a tech-savvy farmer, Steve Collins, with aerial views and details available about the farm crop yield history on his iPad. In the distance I can hear a farm grain elevator likely at the Collins farm filling a silo or bin with corn or soybeans. Grain is sometimes stored before it is marketed at a local grain elevator, likely the Glacial Plains in Murdock, Minnesota, a few blocks from my home. Windy and overcast, low layers of stratus clouds of gray and white blanket the heavens, giving a dark appearance that rain is sure to follow in the next few hours. The fields are wet, so I won't be driving my car into the field, as I seldom do for fear of getting stuck in the mud.

The horizon to the west appears to be almost flat, except for slight rises in the distance. The land is open, almost free from barriers, as this is prairie land. What I am looking at are the remains of the bottom of a glacial lake referred to by archaeologists as Lake Benson, once covering most of Swift County during the late Pleistocene period, about thirteen thousand years ago, according to the Archaeology Lab at Minnesota State University Moorhead. The dirt at Dublin Farm is a dark black prairie soil, ranging from well drained areas, to poorly drained, adding to the complexity of planting and farming soybeans or corn on the "L"-shaped 120 acres. Luckily, Benson drained to a larger glacial lake called Lake Agassiz in the northwest corner of Swift County, covering North America, or there certainly would be no Dublin Farm today. Today there still stands six acres of corn that can't be harvested as the soil is too wet for tractors and combination harvesters, or simply combines, to harvest crops, and it is unknown if remaining crops can be harvested before snow falls.

Before ancient Lake Benson flowed here, glaciers covered Dublin Farm, carrying large stones with the glaciers. There are two piles of fieldstones on the farm, one a small pile about five to six feet tall, if that, located by the old dirt road on the northern portion of the farm. The second pile of fieldstones moved and piled through the years before the start of fall planting is about as high a small barn.

It's not until now I think about the ice covering the land, bringing the stones from the north, Canada or unknown locations. Older homes in Swift County have foundations made from fieldstones, including my home in Murdock, once the location of a flour mill, The Murdock Milling Company. The stone home of Joseph and Anna (Schleh) Schaaf served the location for the first Catholic Masses to be said in the area as early as April 1880 by Father Valentine Stemmler for thirty-seven German Catholic families, and other private homes in the Murdock and vicinity. The stones from the fields are part of Sacred Heart Catholic Church history, not surprising, as stone was a common building material in Ireland, and the materials available to early pioneers on the prairie left behind by the movement of glaciers.

January 2, 2019
Killarney to Dublin, Ireland

I am starting to see the Dublin Bay from my airplane window seat. Originally, I was assigned to an aisle seat, but a lovely Irish traveler next to me could see I was excited about flying from Killarney from the Kerry Airport to Dublin Airport, allowing me to take her window seat.

For most of this flight I've been sleeping on and off, tired from packing my luggage, making sure I left the two-hundred-year old Shamrock Cottage the same as the day I first arrived, December 21, 2018. High in Black Valley, the stone cottage is located in the Gap of Dunloe, more than five miles up a one-track mountain road, separated by the MacGillycuddy's Reeks mountain range in the west, and the Purple Mountain in the east. This morning I drove down the

Gap road, switching lanes back and forth with little traffic, sheep crossing the road as they pleased, passing by the Kate Kearney's Cottage, before finally arriving at the Kerry Airport in Farranfore, in County Kerry around noon. Exhausted, I parked my Passat Volkswagen rental car at Hertz at the Kerry Airport, then rested and fortified myself with a meal from the airport restaurant. There's just one restaurant at this regional Irish airport, and two gates.

From my window seat, looking to the east in Dublin Bay, yellow light fills the sky as the sun sets early in winter at this time, around 4 pm today. Ireland is an island, separated from the continent of Europe, but could be pieced together like a puzzle with the island of Great Britain to the east. From my aerial view I can see the outline of the Wicklow Mountains just south of Dublin. Now I am picking out more colors of blues from the sky and bay, black and gray from the land and mountains, and yellow and orange light is streaming through the clouds toward my airplane window. This is one of the more spectacular views I can remember landing in Dublin, likely as my arrival is so close to the time of sunset.

Buildings, homes, neighborhoods can be defined from the air separated by farm fields and roads, but it's hard to make out exactly what is in view approaching the Dublin Airport. What I do know is the plane is about to land, daylight is escaping, and the landscape is of forty shades of green are blending together while approaching Dublin, the capital city of Ireland.

The landing is very smooth. As I am seated almost in the back row of the aircraft, I'll be one of the first passengers to disembark from this regional commuter. Saying my goodbyes to the smartly dressed Aer Lingus flight crew dressed in green uniforms, I walk down the plane's staircase, and settle my feet on the solid earth of Dublin Airport. I am now in Dublin, Ireland. The name so familiar, it sounds like I am home, almost.

I can't help but take advantage of a photo opportunity standing beside the ATR 72-600 twin-engine turboprop, with a large green shamrock located on the tail the aircraft, obviously for good luck for passengers and flight crew, about seventy passengers in total when completely booked. The shamrock is a symbol of Ireland, and Aer Lingus was once owned by the Irish government. I'm all for large good luck symbols, especially an Irish Shamrock on any aircraft in which I'm a passenger. The airline is Irish, but the regional airliner, ATR is designed by Regional Transport Airplanes, Aerei da Trasporto Regionale, French and Italian, make for a very European flying experience.

January 2, 2019
Brown Thomas
88–95 Grafton Street
Dublin, Ireland

After a taxi ride from the Dublin Airport, I quickly check into my room at the Shelbourne Hotel located on St. Stephen's Green in Dublin. I give myself just enough time to drop my luggage in room 676, and head back on the streets of Dublin, checking with a doorman for directions, even though I knew exactly where I was heading for an evening meal. It's already dark as I walk from St. Stephen's Green with Dubliners filling the sidewalk as they head home from work. I'm walking, turning right on Grafton Street, the same as if I were walking toward Trinity College.

In less than ten minutes, maybe even faster I arrive at Brown Thomas, an Irish department store that originally opened its doors in 1848. I ask a seventy-year-old or so doorman wearing a black top hat and red scarf if the restaurant at the top of the house was still open for the evening. I was in luck, as the store is open until 8 pm. Like a homing pigeon, I started traveling up the escalators to level three, or the fourth floor if measured from an American perspective. I had eaten at the simple, yet elegant European and Irish restaurant on earlier fact-finding genealogy trips and wanted to find my way back for my first day in Dublin.

Sitting down, I notice a familiar face—a young woman from Brazil who worked in the restaurant during my trip in June 2018. Walking toward my table, she greets me with a big smile, and we both say, nearly in unison, our recognition of each other. It's great to see a face in I recognize in Dublin, the largest city and capital of Ireland, with a population of more than 1.2 million people in 2019. I select from the light and bright section of the menu, smoked salmon and avocado toast, served on sourdough bread, with red onions, cress and caper salad. I call my Goduncle Doug, E. Douglas Larson (1926–2022), now in his nineties, from my cellphone while waiting for my food to be delivered. At home in Dublin, and also connected to my family at home in Minnesota, I'm just happy to have an experience that can only be described as delightful and at home on the globe.

❧

It's now about 8:30 pm, and I'm back in room 676 at the Shelbourne watching *The Quiet Man* with John Wayne and Maureen O'Hara, a John Ford movie released in 1952 featuring the Irish countryside. This is not the first time watching this movie, in fact I've watched it countless times, having two copies of the video. What is different about watching this movie is a question that I can't stop thinking about. I wonder if my father's trip to Ireland in 1953 was influenced or promoted by the movie *The Quiet Man*. It's likely my father watched the movie in Benson, Minnesota, at the DeMarce Theatre as my family attended the movies in Benson, recorded in my grandfather's diaries. Could one movie make a young man travel to Ireland? I remind myself my father stayed at the Shelbourne in 1953, though it's unlikely he had a chance to watch TV in his room.

Now very tired, I'm unable to finish watching The Quiet Man. I can smell the dried peat bogs or turf smoke through my window that is open just a crack, the same as I could smell burning turf on Grafton Street. This is Dublin. I'm in Ireland. I'm going to sleep in Dublin city.

January 3, 2019
Shelbourne Hotel
Dublin, Ireland

Waiting for my breakfast to be delivered to my table at the Shelbourne's restaurant I watch pedestrians walk in double or triple time, some pushing strollers and prams, and bicyclists walking past on St. Stephen's Green sidewalks as if they were already late to get to work or first appointments of the day. It's likely there's not a tourist in this morning crowd as there is such a sense of urgency in the forward bending strides, reserved only for someone on a deadline or a clock to beat. The next layer of the street is filled with Dublin's city buses, double-decker tourist buses, cars, motorcycles, scooters and taxis, all part of the continuous circus of Dublin's Fair City. The song of Molly Malone, also known as Cockles and Mussels and In Dublin's Fair City, is an unofficial anthem of Dublin.

St. Stephen's Green is located across the street from the Shelbourne Hotel. The city park takes up twenty-two acres, serving as the playground for local residents and visitors.

I can imagine my father, Martin J. Walsh Jr., in 1953, about twenty-nine, also fascinated by the traffic passing by while eating a full Irish breakfast and sipping a cup of Irish Barry's Tea, maybe thinking of his folks back home in Murdock. After breakfast he would stroll around in St. Stephen's Green park just after the rain stopped on Saturday, May 16, 1953. A Dubliner passing by in the park would snap a photo of Father, smiling with his Clarus 35mm camera, Model MS-35, looking very handsome in his wool brown suit with wide lapels, and pockets stuffed with camera gear, a tiny light meter and extra rolls of Kodachrome. I can only guess the yellow and red flowers are springtime tulips located directly behind my dapper-looking father. The vertical full body portrait is taken for all time, recording my father with his dark hair, thought to be originated from the mixing of the bloodlines of the Irish and Spanish Armada in the 1500s, a theory without solid evidence. If the origins of Black Irish is factual, I'll need to visit Spain, but there's also the Vikings from Northern Europe, Normans, and Gaels, considered to be the Celtic people. Ultimately, it is the rare red hair gene, often noticeable by freckles in people without red hair, passed down by my father and mother, blessing me with red hair, although my father was Black Irish. The theory of Black Irish is something my father told me himself when I was a child, and I have a very vivid memory of him saying the very words of Black Irish.

Shelbourne Eggs Benedict
Two Poached Eggs, Sourdough Muffins
Grilled Irish Fillet of Beef, Hollandaise Sauce

I am eating toast, with orange marmalade served in tiny glass pots from France, with a cup of coffee and orange juice. I'm sure the Irish also have some good marmalades to add to the breakfast table. The French influence of the marmalade could be associated with the waitress calling me Mademoiselle, not Miss or Madam. As I'm planning to walk the streets of Dublin, I ordered the Shelbourne Eggs Benedict, a substantial meal to keep up my strength while touring nearby museums.

I ask for more coffee, and it is delivered in a silver pot. This is one of the finest hotels in all of Dublin and Ireland, as far as I am concerned. I'm sleeping in a room with all white bed linens, complete with a comforter with a border of gold piping embroidered on the front side. The towels are all white, clean, and perfectly hanging nicely with a white robe in the in-suite bathroom. This could only be imagined as a fairy tale to my great-great-grandmother Ellen growing up in rural County Kerry. What would Ellen think of the Shelbourne? Ellen might think they she was in heaven. I have no doubt.

I am looking at St. Stephen's Green as I finish my breakfast. The Georgian era city park was once a marshy land on the edge of Dublin used for grazing livestock until the mid-1600s, and the surrounding area is now filled with buildings and Dublin's main shopping area located just off Grafton Street and surrounding city district.

I wonder if Dublin is too removed from its country roots. There's no place to view a cow in a pasture here, or at least I haven't noticed yet from St. Stephen's Green. There are no sheep grazing these days around the sidewalks of St. Stephen's. The soles of my boots I'm wearing now in the Shelbourne still have tell-tale signs of manure from the Friesian cattle and Scots Black Face Sheep I collected from walking around in rural Killarney. I could not remove the debris as a proper cleaning required a brush. I'm happy to say I'll be walking the streets of Dublin with my honest souvenir attached to my boots from the County Kerry, keeping me very grounded in my family's past. I can think of it as a secret protection from any gobshites in Dublin and beyond.

Now about gobshites, Irish slang, could be considered moderately offensive word, so it must be reserved for special occasions, or not spoken out loud, at least for me. The meaning is a person with poor judgment, or unpleasant character, meaning a gob of excrement, with singular usage, gobshite, and plural, gobshites. It's not my custom to include vulgar language in my daily conversations, but the reality is gobshite could happen if you visit Ireland, and it's best to be prepared, and know the meaning. Simply said, gobshite is Irish for a selfish act, or my meaning I give to this word. I have only encountered the word once during almost half dozen visits to Ireland. An aggressive woman driving a BMW on the narrow mountain roads of the Gap of Dunloe came a few feet away from hitting my VW Passat rental car, or hire car in Ireland, making me back up. I required help from the kind Irish driver behind me to maneuver my car. He immediately said, "What a gobshite that driver is! She could see you couldn't backup properly here, but pushed on." The BMW driver honked at me, causing me to become frazzled. I got out of the car and started to cry, while an Irish woman hugged me. The BMW driver was likely on her way to meet up with clutch of gobshites. This a word I will rarely use, only if I mean it, and maybe not out loud.

January 3, 2019
General Post Office
O'Connell Street Lower
Dublin, Ireland

From the Shelbourne Hotel, a doorman helped me get a taxi to go to O'Connell Street to buy postcard postage stamps at the General Post Office, or GPO for short. Sitting in the front seat, the left side of the taxi, driver on the right, a memory transported me to 1980 as we passed over the River Liffey as traffic slowed to a stop on O'Connell Bridge. Large city buses, double-decker buses and cars needing to get somewhere fast, or maybe they also needed to buy Irish postage stamps like myself.

"Over ahead, that's O'Connell Monument," said the taxi driver.

Dublin taxi drivers seems to always be pointing out tourist points, like you are on a private excursion, and I appreciate that very much.

"Thanks, yes, I know. I can see my Aunt Agnes and Uncle Stanley in 1980 getting out of tour bus somewhere around here, near Clerys, a department store, going shopping. I'm not sure why I remember this so distinctly, but I do. My brother Paul and my Aunt Margaret stayed in the bus and we toured around, picked my aunt and uncle up just about here. It's just like it was yesterday."

I'm can't say why that decisive moment came to mind, but I do have memories from Dublin as teenager. It was my first trip to Ireland; my two aunts and uncle since have passed away. It is known for the big clock in the front of the building as a meeting spot. I have my own memory of Clerys arriving on a flight from Minnesota to Dublin in 2014. My hotel room wasn't ready, and since it is located not far from O'Connell Monument, I walked to Clerys looking for a place to eat and rest. An announcement come over the public address system of a free tea being served, so I enjoyed a pot of gratis tea visiting with ladies from Dublin while watching a demonstration on expensive French cosmetics. I actually remember this was a lovely moment captured in my mind, maybe even better was the conversation, complete with tiny desserts and sandwiches served in two- or three-tiered plates, and Clerys kept serving guests. I'm sure my aunts would have approved of the welcoming tea party served at Clerys, and although I didn't buy any cosmetics, I did get free samples. I visited with the ladies working behind the counters several times at Clerys, chatting about places to visit in Dublin just like I knew them back home in Murdock.

May 1953, my father stood on O'Connell Bridge looking west toward The Customs House, freezing in time with ladies crossing over the River Liffey, and a woman riding a bicycle wearing a dark-colored dress. It's likely he also took the photo of the Daniel O'Connell Monument the same day. O'Connell, 1775 to 1847, was born in County Kerry, and was a politician considered to be the great Catholic Emancipator, starting the process to give civil rights to the Irish in their own country of Ireland ruled by the British. He argued against the Act of Union 1800 that made Ireland and Great Britain the United Kingdom. O'Connell is most known for his meetings attracting crowds of thousands to encourage Ireland to govern itself, free from British rule. In 1922 an Irish Free State Constitution was written, replaced by the current Constitution of Ireland in 1937, leaving the Commonwealth of Nations in 1949, severing ties with Great Britain.

January 3, 2019
College Green at Grafton Street, Trinity College
Dublin, Ireland

I am walking in the College Green located next to Trinity College, old Irish Houses of Parliament, and a statue of Irish patriot Henry Grattan. I'm overwhelmed as I walk through the three-sided plaza with traffic streaming between the sidewalks. The sea of humanity fills the walkable spaces as my ears take in the numerous foreign languages I'm unable to discern. Early Viking kings are thought to be buried in this area. US Presidents Clinton and Obama have addressed crowds in this area. I have my own history related to this green.

My first time walking through College Green was 1980 on my way with family to see the Book of the Kells, an illuminated manuscript of the four Gospels in Latin, at Trinity College. I would not realize until 2019 my father took a photograph in May 1953, almost at the very location where traffic is overwhelming.

Here's what my father wrote on the edge of the Kodachrome slide frame: "Dublin, Ireland, near Trinity College. Note the left-hand drive. May 1953."

With closer inspection of my father's College Green image, I see a road that appears to be dirt or even clay, unpaved, yet difficult to see. An Irish police officer, Garda in Irish, or Guard in English, directs traffic as left-hand driven cars, almost all appearing to be black, except for a Kilmore Dairy truck appearing to be a shade of blue, but it could be how the light is reflecting on the vehicle. At least a dozen men dressed in suits and ties form a lane as they ride bicycles very close to the motorists. A solo bicyclist darts out onto the College Green, very near the curb and not far from where my father was taking his photographs. I can see at least one woman walking her bicycle on the sidewalk, maybe the smartest of all the bicyclists captured in this decisive moment. A sign for Thomas Cook Travel is located on a building in my father's Kodachrome image, today occupied by Tourism Office Dublin on College Green. Pedestrians pack the street. How I would like to know what languages my father was hearing! It's been more than sixty-six years since my father captured this image, and he must have been as overwhelmed with the traffic as me in 2019. In 1953 my father stood in College Green taking photographs with his 35mm camera of this location in Dublin. In 2019 I view College Green and take photos and video with my iPhone that can be slipped in my pocket. The only thing that changed in decades was technology, and my family's curiosity remains constant for capturing images in Dublin.

Dubarry of Ireland, a store located at 35 College Green, Dublin, was my intended destination for the afternoon. I tried on a pair boots, liked them so much, I purchased them and brought them home. They are the boots I keep in my office at St. Cloud State University, and usually wear while teaching. I can easily say my boots are Irish boots, and remind me each time I slip them on that I purchased them at the College Green in Dublin, although the boots were made in Portugal.

January 4, 2019
The National Museum of Ireland Archaeology
Kildare Street, Dublin, Ireland

I just shipped a box with An Post, or The Post, the Irish postal service, of my clothing and other items back home to Murdock before heading to The National Museum of Ireland Archaeology located about a three-minute walk from the Shelbourne. There's many exhibits and a day or two, maybe more, can be spent looking around exhibits of Ireland's Gold, viewing the Tara Brooch, Viking artifacts, inscriptions of early Irish language called Ogham, along with the bell of St. Patrick and its shrine, considered by the museum to be one of the principal relics of Ireland. I can't help but explore the of ancient Irish artifacts when my hotel is just a few blocks away from The National Museum.

After all the preliminary museum touring, I found myself in the Kingship and Sacrifice exhibition. It was my plan to visit the Iron Age bog bodies, along with their sacrificial regalia, hoping to understand the Irish people, likely my ancestors lost in time. Although not all is known about human sacrifices during the Iron Age, the museum states kings of the period were killed and placed along tribal boundaries, and buried in bogs, hence preserving ancient bodies, allowing for historical visits with an ancient Irish man.

In a dark museum exhibit, I am seated on a bench next to the remains of Clonycavan Man, a preserved body of a man dating to the Early Iron Age, 392–201 BC. I see people walk in and out of this secluded room to review his remains found in 2003 by peat cutters in Ballivor, in County Meath, Ireland. The body from the waist down is damaged, but internal organs, and the head remain intact. The dried and mummified body still contains remains of two arms, albeit minus hands. What is most unique is the face appears very recognizable, with an upswept coiffed red hair style, gathered near the forehead, possibly in a tie. Museum information indicates a special hair styling gel from resin likely imported from France or Spain, was used for styling hair.

People continue to walk in and out of the room, something almost like a perpetual funeral, to look at the bog man.

"Let's get out of here." I hear a five- or six-year-old Irish boy say. The boy's father pushes a stroller with a small child concurs with his son. "Let's get out of here quick."

It is likely this bog man was murdered, or part of sacrificial killing, as there's evidence of a series of blows to the head, maybe an ax. Clonycavan Man has red hair, was more than twenty-five years old, and estimated to be no more five feet, nine inches tall and was possibly a king. I am possibly in the presence of royalty, about twenty-three hundred years old. This body was found in a bog on the boundary between the ancient kingdoms of Brega and Mide.

I can't make out everything being said by museum visitors as they are whispering, as if the rosary service would begin shortly at an Irish wake, or what the Irish call a removal, when the body of the deceased is taken from the home to a local Catholic Church. Clonycavan Man was certainly not Catholic or even Protestant, as Christianity didn't exist during the Early Iron Age, and St. Patrick didn't arrive on the island of Ireland from Britain until the fifth century.

A Dutch or maybe a German family speak in English as they encounter the bog man.

"Would his hair be real," asks a little girl.

"Oh yes," her father replies.

"Did his spirit go up to heaven?"

"Oh yes, it could."

Clonycavan Man's housing is some form of protective glass with a metal case sleeping chamber with locks to keep it closed. There are two drawers on the bottom of the housing, similar to a bed with storage compartments. I'd be very surprised if there's linens and blankets tucked away for after the museum closes, a fluffy pillow for a continued long slumber. In this perpetual prehistoric wake, there is no Irish whiskey being toasted, only strangers like myself twisting heads to get a good view. A young man stands near the head of the bog man to sketch a drawing.

What would bog man ask me if he were standing before me, put back together and alive? I think he would ask me about his family and my people. Likely, a discussion about hunting and sources of food. There's no opportunity, only guessing of our conversations, but stories might be told.

As I sit watching Clonycavan Man, I can hear plates being shuffled or cleaned in the Brambles Deli Café at the museum, just a short distance away. I pray a silent prayer before also attempting to sketch the bog man, and head off to the Café for lunch.

January 5, 2019
Shelbourne Hotel, Dublin, Ireland

My luggage is on the bed and I'm trying to pack everything now, so I don't need to rush in the morning as I head to Dublin Airport. I look out through my hotel window to the courtyard and can see an Irish Flag waving in the wind, and I can smell a turf fire burning. I record the moment by taking a few photographs with my iPhone. The sun will set today at 4:20 pm, and this will be my last night in room 676 at the Shelbourne. It's cloudy out. I'm tired. I'm wanting to go home to America.

My Irish roots are certainly here in Ireland. This hotel is part of my father's history as he stayed in room 414, May 12 to 14, 1953, according to the hotel register. A Kodachrome slide taken by my father with his Clarus 35mm, looks out from the Shelbourne, although I am not sure if it was his hotel window. My father labeled the slide, as he did almost his entire trip to Ireland.

"Dublin, Ireland. View from hotel window, Hotel Shelbourne, overlooking St. Stephen's Green, May 1953."

January 6, 2019
Dublin Airport

Note to self in field notebook scribbled at Dublin Airport near elevators to gates: Remember how rude Americans can be in Europe. I remember something very odd going on with an American woman as I waited for an elevator, shoving her luggage and herself in front of me, and leaving me confused. Don't be that person. I can't wait to board the flight home.

March 7, 2019
Murdock, Minnesota

I just picked up my mail at the Post Office in Murdock. The window for business with the post mistress is only open for business during the week until noon and I was expecting packages of books. It's the place to catch up on the latest news around Murdock, second only to Dooley's, the gas station in town.

Slipping into my car to drive the two blocks home, I hear the BNSF railroad engine idling across the street at the grain elevator, likely picking up corn or maybe soybeans to be shipped out to the West Coast, then on to Asian markets. Cars are traveling 30 mph in Murdock on Main Avenue, also known as US Highway 12. If weather was good, I might walk to the Post Office the same as my grandfather Martin to pick up the mail. It's 16 degrees and the sidewalks and roads are icy, with another snowstorm on the way for the weekend, eight to thirteen inches of snow coming at a rate of one to two inches an hour. I can't wait for spring to arrive.

The short BNSF train passes by my house blowing the whistle as it passes through Murdock. Sitting in the living room I look out the window through white sheer curtains. Again, I hear the train whistle blowing, coming from the west, or I could be confused, the east.

I live in the house my father, Martin J. Walsh Jr., was born in 1924, most likely in the front bedroom, as it's been referred to, meaning the only bedroom on the ground floor. I am now the keeper of family headquarters as my aunt Margaret called home. The living room and dining room are separated by formal dark mahogany color columns and woodwork. The sitting room area has the upright piano, sofa, and two large stuffed chairs.

It was likely sometime in the 1970s, maybe 1976, I listened to my father tell the story of belonging to a group called Archbishop John Ireland's people. The pioneering Minnesota Archbishop in the last 1800s established colonies for mainly poor Irish Catholics to start new lives as farmers, with the first colony in De Graff, about three miles west of Murdock. I was a young girl, not yet ten, maybe less, when I heard the story of our family needing to leave the island of Ireland because of food shortages. It is here in Swift County, not far from where I live in Murdock, in rural Dublin Township, my family planted their lives in the United States, eventually becoming US citizens. Surrounding townships in Swift County are named after locations in Ireland, including Cashel, Clontarf, Kildare, Tara, along with other townships named after early settlers from Europe. Shamrocks are found around Murdock, used by many for company logos, including myself for my media and photography business. Riley Bus and Tours send out tour buses around the United States and Canada with huge shamrocks emblazoned on the sides, originating from tiny Murdock.

I can see in the images of my mind my father telling our story to the visitors gathered that day when I was so young, not qualifying for a seat, as the grownups occupied the sofa and chairs, and I was sitting on the floor. My father was the storyteller, and I was the listener.

As much as I want to connect to Dublin, Ireland, it is Dublin Township where I belong. Our family farm, not the family's original homestead, is often called Dublin Farm. I might have grown up in Litchfield, Minnesota, my official hometown, where my father worked as a telegrapher and station manager for the Great Northern and Burlington Northern Railroad, but it is Murdock I am deeply rooted in history. Sacred Heart Catholic Cemetery, about one house away from the west end of Murdock on Highway 12, is filled with my family and ancestors, four or five generations, serving as a personal genealogy outdoor archive if I need to check a spelling, birth or date of death. St. Bridget's Catholic Cemetery in De Graff has the oldest of the original settlers buried for my family. Murdock and De Graff have large Celtic crosses in the graveyards like found in Ireland.

Another freight train is passing through Murdock heading west, fairly short, less than a dozen rail cars. I can't help but stop what I am doing to look out the window.

Dublin Township in Murdock, Minnesota is home. I have a Blackthorn Shillelagh hanging in the kitchen for good luck, or if I need to use it as a weapon. There's usually an old sickle tucked away by the front door, like you see used years ago to cut the grass.

The fieldstone foundation of my house was once a flour mill. I live in this small white wooden house my family has called home since early 1922. It is here I rest at night, safely in my bed in the front room. I can call Dublin in Ireland a place I know and can't wait to visit again. When I'm in Dublin city, Ireland, I want to come home to Dublin Township in Swift County, Minnesota. Freight cars are now moving on the rail tracks outside and the train whistle is sounding again. All of this is how I know I am home.

Epilogue

April 9, 2021
Sacred Heart Cemetery
Murdock, Minnesota

IT IS RAINING AS I WALK HOLDING AN UMBRELLA IN my right hand and leash to my dachshund in the other, wearing my green waterproof trench coat and waterproof boots, the very same I wore in Ireland visiting Townland Dromkerry where my family once lived and worked. The rain prompted me for some reason to walk in the cold, 43 degrees with winds almost 20 mph, to Sacred Heart Cemetery, just more than one house away from my home. It's weather for a fool to take a walk in today.

During my quest to find the roots of my Irish ancestors, I spent a lot of time searching in cemeteries, walking in the footsteps of my ancestors and Saint Colman at Killagha Abbey in County Kerry, Ireland. Walking westward on the sidewalk along Main Avenue, I see a blue canopy tent with guideline ropes to cover the temporary structure over a small open grave for today's mourners. There will be a burial today. Walking through the center road of the cemetery, just north over to the location of the large Irish crosses of early settlers and parish priests, I see an open farm field ready for spring planting, likely for corn or soybeans. East toward the corner of Orleans Street and Clara Avenue, about two blocks away is Sacred Heart Catholic Church, surrounded by parked cars on the street. Any moment a funeral procession could be arriving, thus I hasten my pace in the rain. Funerals now are very private during the pandemic, family only. The weather is foul, and I'm already wanting to return home. A Riley's tour bus with huge shamrocks painted on the sides of its carriage departs a service garage, and travels east down Clara Avenue toward the church. The people of Murdock have not forgotten their Irish past.

I walk even faster past graves of my ancestors bearing names of Walsh, Foley, and McGinty, some directly from Ireland, Scotland, Luxembourg, Canada and more. I want to visit my parents, grandparents, Aunt Margaret, and baby brother David. After almost losing my umbrella in a gust of wind, I quickly pray at their gravesites. My small dachshund wearing a winter coat walks on the wet and muddy green grass above where my family rests. This is my first visit in 2021 to the cemetery, a short one as now I want to go home.

Since returning from my last trip to Ireland, January 2019, I've learned William Foley, my great-great-grandfather, was able to use the stars in the sky to navigate, celestial navigation. The folklore of William's ties to the town of Killorglin, in County Kerry, Ireland, and now the connection of navigation have even more meaning. Killorglin is very close to Castlemaine Harbour, flowing first to Dingle Bay, then out to the North Atlantic Ocean. Knowledge of navigation would seem to be a good fit living so close to water in the west of Ireland.

The graves I walked past quickly included my great grandparents, Stephen F. Foley, born in Calais, Maine, 1846–1913, and Catherine Meier Foley, born in Luxembourg, 1855–1921.

William as young man in Ireland, learned to direct the sailing of his ships with a compass, viewing the stars to determine his direction. This alone tells me my family has ties to the sea and its adventures. The Murdock Centennial 1878–1978, lists the Foley history as follows in regard to William, "He was the descendant of a long line of sailors, tracing back to the Vikings, and his ability to navigate was handed down through the generations." I didn't know this information about William as a child, my father never told me this story or perhaps didn't have any knowledge, but I am very happy to share these details, especially to preserve for future generations. As far as connections to the Vikings, they certainly had a tradition of raiding, trading, followed by settling, in this case Ireland. The red-hair gene from the Vikings or potential of lineages all add to my genetic makeup and red hair.

When Stephen, along with his brothers, and father William, traveled to the Murdock area to see his homestead, navigation by stars was used. It was September 10, 1883, Stephen received the first patent for the land of his homestead, followed by another in 1895, according to Homestead records with the US Department of the Interior, Bureau of Land Management. Needing at least five years to prove up or make improvements to his land, the year 1878 or thereabouts was likely when William, about age fifty-six, used his star navigation skills to help find home. The story goes on to say the railroad line ended at that time in Willmar, so he needed to walk the next twenty miles. In checking facts about the railway, by 1869 the

St. Paul and Pacific railroad, according to *Swift County Minnesota: A Collection of Historical Sketches and Family,* already reached as far as Willmar, and arrived in Benson in 1870, meaning the railroad was already passing through Murdock area. The story indicates the sons of William wanted to wait until morning, and break their travel as it was a dark and cloudy night. William insisted they walk to their homesteads in the area of Louriston Township, in Chippewa County, just south of Dublin Township in Swift County. William "led the boys" directly to the sod house on Stephen's land, arriving in the middle of the night. Stephen's brothers, James G. Foley and William F. Foley Jr., also had homesteads in Chippewa County, and were likely part of the night navigation expedition to Louriston. It's unfortunate the author of this story was not recorded, but it is certainly a story worth cherishing. The idea of walking twenty miles in the night, using only stars in the sky as a guide, makes me very proud to know more about the character of my people. William must have thought of his sons owning their own land as a miracle. He left behind his old world in Ireland where Catholics were not landowners, instead tenants of English Protestants.

In spring of 1878, Catherine and Stephen were both living on the homestead in Louriston, moving from Stillwater, Minnesota. This homestead is where they lived the rest of their lives, and where my grandmother Jennie Foley Walsh was born, 1886. The Foley's early years were difficult as pioneers, as they lost their first two crops to hail and grasshoppers, according to Foley family history.

The grasshopper plague, according to James Patrick Shannon, "Catholic Colonization on the Western Frontier," destroyed crops at least two years in the De Graff area, 1876 and 1877. Local Catholic pioneers joined with Archbishop John Ireland in 1876 on the streets to pray in De Graff in a procession of the Blessed Sacrament during the grasshopper plague. When all else fails, then it's by faith and prayer where strength is found, as the same applies today.

When the grasshoppers came again 1877, Father John McDermot, parish priest of De Graff, acted quickly, buying a hopperdozer for the farmers, a large steel, scooped machine filled with tar, drawn by horses in the fields, not causing damage to the crops. McDermot arranged with the St. Paul and Pacific Railroad delivery free of charge from St. Paul all the coal tar needed to trap the grasshoppers.

I am from a line of people who left their old worlds behind, deliberately moved to this Minnesota prairie with blizzards in the winter, snow covering their temporary shanty homes on their homesteads, and plagues of grasshoppers destroying crops in their early years as settlers, yet know how to use stars in the sky to find a sod house in the dark of night. I am proud and lucky to be of this line of hearty and tenacious stock of people.

***

As I start to leave the cemetery, I see my first male American robin of the year very close to the open grave, giving a sign spring has arrived, and better yet, giving hope to a difficult and painful time for mourners at this very location today. It's a bit hard to make out the orange-red breast as the rain comes down stronger, but I'm able to detect a distinct yellow bill, knowing for certain it's a robin.

Looking back where my family rests not far from the pine trees, I think about how their lives were swept up years, decades or centuries before today. I think again about how the farmland surrounding Murdock plays a significant role in my life. Just beyond the cemetery and rows of pine trees, on the edge of the farm fields, looking west at the summer sunset, it's the edge of the world, and entrance to heaven, all not far from the steps of my front porch. In the winter, it's a curtain of snow during blizzards, cutting off the world, and all travel. This location, especially when the sun is setting, and corn is higher than my knees, several feet above my head in summer, I think I am in one of the most extraordinary locations on earth. I'm at home in Murdock.

Today in Murdock, my priority is to keep healthy and safe during a global pandemic started in March 2020. Travel today involves trips to area grocery stores in nearby Kerkhoven, Benson, and Murdock, wearing a protective face mask. One day, when the world moves past this pandemic, life might be altered in ways not yet revealed to us.

In 2021, travels I made to Ireland almost two and half years ago would not be happening today due to the pandemic. Traveling twice in one year to Ireland, May and early June 2018 and December 2018 and early January 2019, seemed so imperative, if not required at the time in my quest. Looking back now with current travel restrictions, and Ireland's protective lockdowns, my thoughts are validated as wise travel decisions.

During my last days in Dublin in January 2019, staying at the Shelbourne Hotel, I wanted to depart Ireland, as I was exhausted, cold, worn out. I also believed I've tied as many loose ends together as possible, and work was complete. Something I believe to be true today, but always look forward to any new information, and research.

Now in Murdock, and walking in the rain, and I just want to be in my warm and comfortable, small wooden white house of more than a century, a place Aunt Margaret called headquarters. Here at headquarters the world makes even more sense in the pandemic, not to mention political and economic unrest, nationally and around the world. Walking back home from the cemetery, I wonder if I will encounter the funeral procession as it's likely to pass by my home on Main Avenue.

In the safety of my home this last year, I learned of pandemic deaths, sometimes compared to the total dead of past wars, racial unrest around the world, including Minnesota, and an attempted insurrection in Washington DC of the United States on my birthday, January 6, 2021.

On a personal level, keeping safe at home has encouraged creativity, and desire to explore more stories. The pandemic has taught me the significance of finding and preserving family stories. It might be exactly these trying times when the trials of such stories are forgotten in order to survive beyond the current day and future generations.

A century ago my grandparents Martin and Jennie Walsh, along with Aunts Agnes and Margaret, my father not yet born, weathered the storms of the 1918–1919 global Spanish influenza pandemic. A year or so before Aunt Margaret died, she mentioned to me she survived this part of history, living with her family in a hotel in Murdock, the typical living arrangement as houses were built for the new village.

My brother Paul, about age five or six in 1966, heard conversations at the house of our grandparents in Murdock about the same year, 1966, Walt Disney died, the American animator. William Joseph Foley (1883–1971), brother of Grandma Jennie, could be overheard by young Paul talking about the Spanish influenza pandemic and their worries about going out of the house to buy food, and more.

My family glides through history, sometimes encountering the famous or infamous people along the way. About the same year Paul remembers conversations about the epidemic, another event happens with him and our dad at the now former Curtis Hotel in Minneapolis.

"I got to see Richard Nixon up close in 1966 at the Curtis Hotel in Minneapolis. Dad and I were standing at the elevator, and whole lot of guys walked out. Dad told me that it was Richard Nixon."

I can't say when my ancestors arrived on the island of Ireland or if they walked on ice and snow bridges when the world's land was still emerging from glaciers. My travels to finding Dromkerry and Knockanaroor are the closest locations to the epicenter of my Irish roots. Survival is the best possible answer in one word to describe reasons for leaving Ireland, and making home in Murdock, Dublin Township in Swift County, Minnesota.

I am waiting for water in the kettle to boil on the stove, and drink a cup of hot Earl Grey tea. A lot of tea has been made in this old kitchen at headquarters in the past century, and a lot more to come.

July 10, 2021
St. Bridget's Catholic Cemetery
De Graff, Minnesota

Final notes: Today I am walking around St. Bridget's Catholic Cemetery in De Graff searching for a grave of a Foley family member, but I'm having no luck. Instead, I find graves I've searched for at least ten years. Just as I'm getting ready to head back to my car, I discover the graves of my great-great-grandparents Michael John Walsh Sr., 1812–1901, from County Kilkenny, Ireland, and Catherine Summers Walsh, 1833–1909, also from Ireland, but her specific location or townland is unknown. I've enlisted help in the past to find these graves, but always came up short. Now that I've found the location in the southwest section of the cemetery, I understand why I had difficulty. How did I miss this five- or six-foot-tall memorial to my great-great-grandparents? First, the graves are away from view of the main north-south cemetery road. From the road, only the east side of monument is in view, with no inscriptions facing the dirt cemetery road, inscriptions only on the west side of marker. The inscriptions are very faint on the sandstone, weathered during the last 120 years of exposure to Minnesota prairie weather. I am sure I've walked past these graves numerous times, but it was today I found their resting location.

I have not been able to discover as many details of my Walsh family's origins in County Kilkenny as my Foley family history in County Kerry. There are no records found of Michael's mother or father, simply lost in time, at least for now. A generation is considered about twenty years, making the time of his parents' births about 1792, but only an estimate.

As I was so excited to find their grave today, I decided to search for a marriage record online from Catholic church records in Kingston, Ontario, Canada. My Irish luck helped me find their marriage records around midnight just before enjoying a chicken sandwich. I thought I was close to finding the marriage record, and couldn't stop searching.

Michael and Catherine married at the Cathedral of St. Mary of the Immaculate Conception in Kingston, Ontario, Canada, November 2, 1857. The couple lived on Wolfe Island, a small island located near Kingston, reached by ferry from Canada and the United States. My great-grandfather Michael John Walsh Jr. (1858–1929) was born in Canada, likely Kingston or Wolfe Island, along with his brothers and sisters, eight children total, before moving to Minnesota. There's a few hints in the handwritten marriage record that might jump start future investigations about my Walsh family roots, but I'll need time, and must enlist help.

My great-great-grandfather Michael, according to his 1901 obituary married his first wife, Mary Moran, in 1829 in Ireland, and she died in 1831, leaving one son named Patrick Walsh. Bridget Moran, second wife of Michael Sr., appears for the first time in modern family history in 2021. She is recorded in the marriage record, 1857, as the late wife to my great-great-grandfather Michael Sr., listed as a widower. Bridget died earlier in 1857, the same year Michael Sr. married third wife Catherine Summers, my great-great-grandmother. Bridget is buried at the old Catholic Cemetery on Wolfe Island. Patrick was mentioned in his father's obituary as residing in Philadelphia, and first in the series of nine children mourning for his father.

Today I found a gravesite of my Irish born great-great-grandparents only a few miles away from home at the De Graff cemetery, along with a marriage record that recently become available online in 2021. My own father did not know the details of the marriage of his great grandparents. Just when I thought all the possible avenues were exhausted, there's more details to explore.

As I am winding up my book, I imagine one day visiting St. Mary's Cathedral in Kingston and taking the ferry to Wolfe Island, exploring where my family walked this Earth in Canada before finding home here in Dublin Township.

Final Irish Blessing

As the Irish have countless blessings for encountering struggles, seeking hope and comfort, desiring better futures, I offer the following as an improvised Irish blessing, with a bit of Irish wit, maybe my greatest Irish treasure.

May God extend blessings to all readers of this book.
May readers find and tell stories of their Irish ancestors as a gift to future generations.
May all Irish descendants in the Irish Diaspora call Ireland home, if not in some small way.
May you not fall asleep while reading this book, but occasional rests are just fine.

About the Author

Jannet L. Walsh, Murdock, Minnesota-based photographer, author, educator, is a first-time published author of a creative nonfiction quest about her Minnesota and Irish heritage. Walsh received a 2022–2024 McKnight Foundation Grant for writing about her family's Irish Canadian roots on Wolfe Island, Ontario, Canada, in the middle of the St. Lawrence River.

In this endeavor, Walsh combines Irish family detective skills with creative nonfiction narration. Readers imagine they are walking with her in rural Minnesota, in Ireland, and in Canada, in her "you are there" writing genre, inherited from her family's oral tradition.

Walsh has written on technology, travel, religion, and was a newspaper columnist on career, workforce, and business. Her writing appears in IrishCentral. com as a correspondent on topics related to the Irish Diaspora. Her photos and videos have been featured by CNN, CNN iReport, HLN, The New York Times Company and the California Academy of Sciences. Walsh served as assistant professor of strategic communications and multimedia at St. Cloud State University. She holds a Master of Arts from Ohio University in photography, and Master of Fine Arts in Creative Writing from Augsburg University. *Higgledy Piggledy Stones: Family Stories from Ireland and Minnesota* is her first book.

SHANTI ARTS

NATURE · ART · SPIRIT

Please visit us online
to browse our entire book catalog,
including poetry collections and fiction,
books on travel, nature, healing, art,
photography, and more.

Also take a look at our highly regarded art
and literary journal, *Still Point Arts Quarterly*,
which may be downloaded for free.

www.shantiarts.com

www.ingramcontent.com/pod-product-compliance
Lightning Source LLC
Chambersburg PA
CBHW020533270326
41927CB00006B/555